AF616571

INTERNATIONAL MONEY AND CAPITAL

SUKUMAR NANDI

BUSINESS PUBLICATIONS INC

ISBN 81-86982-77-9

Cover design Akshay Dange

Published by
BUSINESS PUBLICATIONS INC
229/A 2nd Floor, Krantiveer Rajguru Marg
Girgaon Mumbai 400 004
Tel 380 8817 / 380 8819 Fax 387 2625

CONTENTS

PREFACE

This is a book of international money, finance and capital, an important area of applied economics in the modern day world. For the last six years while participating in the discussions in different forums including the workshops at the National Institute of Bank Management (NIBM), I have the feeling that the economics of international flow of money and capital should be placed in proper perspective. Also the world financial system has been transforming at a quicker pace and the integration of the system is much more than what most of us are accustomed to think. This book is an attempt to analyse this aspect in a theoretical perspective. The latter does not become perfect and objective unless some sort of quantification is attempted. With this belief the relevant economic models have been discussed and empirical estimations have been made on the basis of up to date data. That way Chapters III, IV and V have been good exercises in applied econometrics.

Regarding the coverage of the book, Chapters I and II give the reader a broad introduction to the type of subjects dealt in the later part of the book. The concept of money has undergone revolutionary changes in recent times and that has been discussed in Chapter I. It is shown in this chapter how space and time are related with the concept of money in modern day world. The second chapter is complementary to the first in the sense that here money has been focussed in the international perspective. The structure of the international financial regime and different institutions have been discussed. Also the mechanism of the international money has been analysed in brief. Meanwhile a new currency has come into existence on January 1, 1999 in the name EURO and a full discussion on that has been placed in the Appendix.

We are passing through a phase of brainstorming for the search of the real causes of the type of financial meltdown in some Asian countries. Though final judgement is yet to come, the trickles which are coming out of South Korea, Thailand and other countries point to at least two aspects and these are–unrestricted capital flow in the private sector and the inability of the countries to maintain adequate international reserves to manage the liquidity problem. While the Asian countries have provided the case study materials, economists for a long time have been doing research on the impact of capital flow across the political boundaries. This mobility of capital and the spatial dimenion of money have fascinated me for a long time. As mentioned above, the Asian crisis is still unfolding. A short discussion of the Asian crisis has been placed in Appendix with the belief that readers being briefed by the theoretical framework in the main chapters of the book will find this as a good case study of capital mobility as well as capital flight.

The core of the book starts from Chapter III where international capital mobility is dealt in greater detail. The Feldstein-Horioka model is the theoretical structure on which the relevant hypothesis of saving-investment correlation has been tested on the basis of data of several countries including India. While capital moves across the political boundaries, it has another implication in the form of flight of capital. The latter takes place generally from the countries where it is needed most, i.e. the poor developing countries. A model is built from the theories in the literature and then it has been estimated to determine and quantify the determinants of capital flight. The information about the determinants will facilitate the formulation of the policies to check the flight of capital. The last chapter deals with the demand for international reserve. As mentioned above one group of economists are of the opinion that the cause of the financial turmoil in south Asia is that the concerned countries failed to maintain adequate international reserve to manage the liquidity crisis. From this angle the theoretical underpinnings of the holding of the international reserve on the part of a country are important to study.

This is not a text book, but this can be a good complementary reference book on international finance for the students in postgraduate classes both in the universities and management schools. Also this book will be a good companion for researchers, professionals and executives in the international divisions of banks.

Every book is a cooperative effort and this one is no exception. The first idea of this book originated when I had been writing my Ph.D. dissertation at Utah State University in the area of international finance. I had been benefitted through discussion with the professors of Economics department and specially I am indebted to Dr. Basudeb Biswas, who as the Supervisor of my Ph.D. dissertation encouraged me to remain alert about the related subjects. I also acknowledge my debt to Dr. Kenneth Lyon for his critical view and love for mathematics, to Dr. Cris Lewis for his encouragement. Also colleagues of Economics departments of Vidyasagar University and Calcutta University and at the National Institute of Bank Management have been kind enough to offer comments on earlier drafts of some of the topics discussed in this book. I am indebted to them. The students of postgraduate classes in the Economics departments of Vidyasagar University and Calcutta University and the participants of the workshops held at different times at the National Institute of Bank Management helped to clarify certain ideas through discussions. I am indebted to them. I am also indebted to several young persons–Paromita Bhattacharya, Bikash Apte, Megha Jayadevan, Manisha Bhosale and Arati Waiker–as they have helped in the research work by the collection and analysis of data, and also in the correction of proofs of the manuscripts at various levels. I acknowledge my debt to them. I am also indebted to Mrs. Kumud Lagu who wordprocessed the whole manuscript and brought it to its present form.

I would like to thank Mr. Jai Saxena, Managing Director, and Mrs. Chandralekha Maitra, Editor of Business Publications Inc. for their keen interest and endeavour in bringing out this book within a very short time.

Finally I acknowledge my debt to my wife, Karabi and daughters, Susmita and Nabanita who had to bear the opportunity cost of time as I remained busy with the book. Of course, the usual disclaimer applies as I alone remain responsible for the errors in the book.

Sukumar Nandi
National Institute of Bank Management
Pune

I

MONEY, POWER AND SPACE : GLOBAL ORIGIN

"Money speaks sense in a language all nations understand."

Aphra Behn (1682)

THE PROGRESS OF HUMAN CIVILIZATION has been associated with a continuous interaction among different groups of human beings across the continents. This brings some cultural evolution in the sense that sharp ethnic differences get blunted. One important aspect of the modern civilization is its strength to impose homogenization across political boundaries and also over time. In this complex process the invention of money in the history of mankind has been beneficial. This role of money has been appreciated by the philosophers starting from Karl Marx in the 19th century to very recently Zelizer (1994). The arguments in the traditional social philosophy is that the evolution of money over the ages has been associated with a revolutionary shift in the nature of social relations, which has replaced personal bonds with a formal relation based on materialistic considerations. As an important socio-economic institution money performs some functions which modern theory has stylized like the following :

First, money acts as a unit of account, that is as a medium which serves as the base of the accounting system.

Second, money acts as a common measure of value, as a numeraire of the valuation of the commodities for exchange against each other or against the money.

Third, money performs the role of medium of exchange by performing the role of a unit of account and a measure of value. Also the ability of money in the exchange processes means that it becomes a common universal equivalent, which can be exchanged for all other commodities including the monies of other places.

Fourth, the three roles of money, i.e., the unit of account, measure of value and medium of exchange, make it a store of value in an exchange system. Thus money becomes an index of the stock of wealth to the private economic agents.

The store of value function of money explains the strength of money to build bridges between places distant in space and time. It has replaced the system of barter, and thus the double coincidence of wants is no longer necessary for exchange becoming effective between two economic agents at two distant places without knowing each other, and money works in between. This evolution of money-based economic exchange has brought about a homogenization of economic space, which has been described as "disembedding" (Giddens, 1990).[1] The latter is explained as a process where the spread of institution and practices associated with modern life has changed longstanding social practices in the local places, and in this way the monetization of the economy has helped to move social life away from the rigidity of tradition.

Through the historical sweeps of time the evolution of money had been swift starting from commodity money in the earlier times to the present day plastic money where commodity transfer and monetary transactions take place in parallel fashion without the actual use of money, thanks to the development of computer and information technology. While the latest 'avatar' of money has far reaching implications to be discussed later, the creations of money has led to the homogenization of space within the political boundaries of a nation state. The creation of this national financial space had been the mainstay of the development of the state system between the 16th and the 19th centuries. This paved the way for the foundation of the capitalist system. Also national financial space was based upon the circulation of "fiduciary" money, that means money having no intrinsic value like commodity money, but is guaranteed through the state's supervision and surveillance of the national financial system, which may vary from place to place. For the stability of the financial system the state is to frame rules and regulations which the institutions are to comply (Giddens, 1985). The process for the compact formation of national financial space had taken long years in some cases. As for example, though Bank of England was in 1694, it was not until the 19th century that it began to open branch network throughout England and effectively started controlling the monetary system.

The compactness of the national financial space started showing the signs of crack in the closing decades of the 20th century through a process what is now known as "deterritorialization". The process of homogenization has led to the situation where the distinctiveness of national financial space has been eroded, as is seen in the equilization of interest rates and the finance capital becoming much more powerful which dwarfs other economic parameters showing the distinctiveness of the national economies (Corbridge, 1994). When a conscious effort is made on the convergence of domestic interest rate with the world one, it amounts to bringing the time preference of the citizens at par with people of other countries.

As mentioned above, the evolution of electronic or plastic money is not tied to the nation state as the fiduciary issue is. The international credit card issued by companies such as Visa, Mastercard etc. represent a new form of money, which empowers the holders of such cards the ease of movement across different financial spaces. This induces the need to transform one category of currency into another for the movement of money across political boundaries. All these are run by some big financial institutions, who operate beyond the national financial space and at transnational scale. The activities of these institutions have serious implications for the local institutions, who are overwhelmed by the practices of the big transnational financial institutions operating from big financial centres through a complex network and often using languages which are full of symbols. Today we find some immense powerful financial centres that consists of a network of big financial institutions and markets and these radiate power on a global market (Thrift, 1994). Unless some form of insularity exists for the local financial space, the shock waves emanating from the powerful financial centres can destabilize the local financial system.

Sometimes it is argued that the globalization of money funds often leads to the end of geography as a result of the demise of the nation state as the single most important institution to control and regulate the value of money. Money is always on the move and it must go somewhere (O'Brien, 1991). One implication of this is that to the same extent the authority loses control on the monetary policy it wants to pursue.

Money constitutes social relationship between people. The different connotations of the operation of monetary process and also the determination of the value of money are shaped and also transformed through social relations. Again, holding of money breeds social power. As sociologists argue money lies at the centre of "power geometry" of socio-spatial relations between economic agents and its complex web of relations of subordinations (Massey, 1993). The social characteristics of money make it an instrument of oppression for some persons and for others this can be the source of power and control. This is also related to the social geography of the money process.

Karl Marx (1867) developed the theory of money as a critique of the ideas of earlier writers like Hume and Ricardo. He argued that the prices of commodities in a commodity money systems were prior to the quantity of money, and therefore the quantity theory of money and price level was not correct. Also he rejected the Say's Law as explained by Ricardo (1811) on the ground that the movement of money into and out of the hoards was asymmetric and as money reflects the demand in the real sector, it might create a difference between the aggregate supply of the goods and their aggregate demand. Further, Marx argued that the quantity of money commodity should be viewed as endogenous to the economic system and he emphasized the distinction between the effects of exogeneous issues of non convertible paper money and the endogenous movement of the money commodity. It is also true that Marxian scheme of money as a social relation emphasized the primacy of production decisions constrained by the accumulation of capital in controlling the level of economic activity of the society.

KEYNES AND MODERN VERSION OF MONEY The theory of money as developed by Keynes (1936) was the academic response to the drastic changes in the world economic scene after World War I. In the Keynesian money system central bank remains at the centre and its liabilities may or may not be convertible into a money commodity. The liabilities of the central bank serve as the reserve of the commercial banks, who again issue deposits. Keynes deals with the question how the financial system does absorb the reserves of the deposits created by banking system. He has argued that the rates of return on the competing monetary assets like bonds and equities must adjust until wealth holders are satisfied to hold these assets and deposits in the proportion in which these assets are being supplied to the public. In the process a change in the reserve policy of the central bank induces a change in the rates of return to the bonds and equities. Again the latter determine the cost of capital funds to the firms, and so the changes in these return do alter the incentives of the firms to make any longterm investment decision. An increase in the bank reserves induces a fall in the interest rates, which again encourages investment by the firms and the multiplier effects of the latter increases the overall economic activity. Thus there exists a strong relation between the reserve creation of the central banks and the level of economic activity.

Keynesian monetary framework as explained briefly above provided the theoretical perspective on which later theorists developed their models. The basic elements like a demand function for money with arguments like income, wealth and rates of return of different assets, an exogeneous supply of money, and the connection between money and real activity through changes in the rates of return and prices of money and non-money assets became the common elements of the new quantity theory of money developed in post-Keynesian period by Milton Friedman, James Tobin and others.

MUNDELL-FLEMING FRAMEWORK AND OPEN ECONOMY MACROECONOMICS Robert Mundell (1971) has extended the Keynesian framework of money into the open economy. In the latter if the currency is fully convertible and floating, the supply of domestic money is no longer exogeneous. When the central bank expands the money supply, the citizens may react in such a way that they exchange domestic monetary claims for international reserve assets to offset the expansion of money supply. This implies the movement of capital out of the country. Thus in an open economy with fully convertible exchange rate of the domestic currency, the domestic capital market becomes open to the world, and the rates of return of domestic assets will converge to the world rates of return adjusted to the rates of changes of the exchange rates.

So a change in the supply of money domestically will influence the exchange rate through its effects on the price level and the interest rates. In this framework a central bank can change the economic activity in the short run by expanding the supply of money, which reduces the interest rates and the latter induces expansion in the economic activity. But over time domestic price level adjusts having its impact on the exchange rates and the resultant capital movements. Thus the short run effects dissipate in the long run. This effectiveness of monetary policy in the short run has been challenged by Lucas (1981) when he brings the rational expectation framework and argues that the activities of the economic agents will offset the short-term gain the authorties expect to bring in the economy.

Fleming (1962) dealt with similar problem as done by Mundell, and later on, this has been known in the literature as Mundell-Fleming framework and an integrated form is available in Frenkel and Razin (1987). The latter has explained the different scenario of the impact of fiscal policies on the parameters of the economy framework. As explained by Frenkel and Razin (1987) in a general equilibrium framework under a fixed exchange rate regime an increase in government expenditure financed by taxation shall induce a balance of payments deficit and reduce both shortterm and longterm money holdings. On the contrary, if the increasing government expenditure is financed by the creation of debt, it shall lead to a surplus in the balance of payments and both shortterm and longterm money holding will rise. Clearly, as the exchange rate remains fixed, the fiscal expansion in the economy is having its fall out through the changes in the balance of payments. Also, when fiscal expansion is financed by the creation of public debt, the Theory of Ricardian equivalence 2 induces the economic agent to save more for the future as the redemption of debt shall call for fresh taxation. This increasing saving is reflected in the surplus in the balance of payments. This shall lead to an appreciation of the exchange rate if the exchange rate becomes flexible.

One import of the Mundell-Fleming model is that in the fully integrated world economy the transmission mechanism across the political boundaries operate through the interest rates, as the direction of the capital flow from the country shall depend on the relative real interest rate of the country. Again, the changes in the nominal interest rates induce the dynamics of the changes in the exchange rate of the domestic currency. This aspect is very important in understanding the dynamics of the recent South-Asian crisis, which has been chracterised by large scale capital flow and exchange rate depreciation.

The classical economists started with the premise that money is a 'veil', implying the neutrality of money. The South-Asian experiences have shown that disturbances in the money market can spill over to the real segments of the economy and can create serious problem in the real sector. The development of the world capitalism has become much more complex and it demands greater attention from the academics.

Global Money Since the breakdown of the Bretton Woods System the world financial market has witnessed two distinct phases. First, the evolution of the petroleum cartel of the Organization of the Petroleum Exporting Countries (OPEC) in the early seventies led to the parking of billions of euro dollars in European banks. This induced the growth of international banking in the late seventies and international capital flows started in a big way as some countries within OPEC could not absorb fully their inflated export earnings and preferred to invest the money in European and American banks. This phase also witnessed the demise of the fixed exchange rate system which had been part and parcel of the Bretton Woods System. Thus flexible exchange rate system emerged and the members of International Monetary Fund started the new realignment of their currencies vis-a-vis U.S. dollar.

The second phase started in the middle of the eighties when international banking witnessed the disintermediation process and the emergence of the large fund managers in the international capital market. International capital mobility also increased along with the volatility of the exchange rate of major currencies. The latter happened as U.S. dollar weakened. A flexible exchange rate system, a large increase in the international flow of capital and a weak U.S. dollar created conditions for the swift interchange of currencies across the political borders. The growth of some large centres of international financial market and some offstore centres accentuated this process. Thus the world for the first time started to witness the large scale trading in currencies, which were not related to the international transaction in commodities.

Starting from the middle of the eighties major currencies of the world started to fluctuate in relative value against each other depending on the combination of national economic policies and international capital flows. Sometimes attempts had been made to regulate the flow of money but these could not succeed. There had been a tremendous growth of global 'hot' money and this development had a parallel with the expansion of the offstore financial centres. The importance of the latter can be measured by the report that about 50 per cent of the world's stock of money either resides in, or pass through these offstore financial centres, which make these centres important catalyst for world trade (Johns, 1994). These centres face less control and a very relaxed tax system. The result has been that they regulate huge amount of stateless money through 24-hour trading. The deregulation of the money markets both in the U.S.A. and England gave a spurt to the expansion of the global financial markets so much so that by the end of 1993 total gross international bank liabilities stood at U.S. $ 7.3 trillion (BIS, 1994).

The volatility of the exchange rate of major currencies and the deregulation in the international financial centres created immense opportunities for arbitrage operations. This induced a tremendous increase of trading in currencies. The latter became an important vehicle of accumulation of capital as foreign exchange market grew from a modest figure of U.S. $ 15 billion in 1970 on a single day to an astronomical figure of U.S. $ 1.6

trillion per day towards the close of 1996. The lion's share of this volume is driven by constant hedging, arbitrage and speculative transaction for position taking in the international financial markets. The financial centres in the U.S.A., U.K. and Japan accounted for about 60 per cent of the trading of currencies in 1994. One interesting aspect of these deals is that almost all these involve spatial transfer of money along with the changes in the exchange rates of the nations' currencies. The transfers are often motivated by the possibilities of the changes in the relative values of the currencies, and often the causality runs both ways.

The increased volume of transactions has induced certain changes in the international financial market. The latter is equipped now with sophisticated computer network which on the one hand provides uptodate information regarding the market which analyses and helps transactions across the globe within minutes. The development of information technology has helped the process. It is now possible to move money to banks in the farthest corner of the globe within a very short time. This sort of time-space transaction through the computer based telecommunication system has allowed an on-the-spot market equilibrium. Swift movement of money matches demand with supply by the change in the exchange rate.

Another interesting aspect is the growing importance of the forward transactions in the total volume of daily turnover. The importance of the spot market had been supreme in the early seventies, but by 1989 the share declined to 57 per cent, and it declined further to 47 per cent in 1992 (BIS,1993). The increasing importance of the forward transaction is due to increasing position-taking for pure speculation in the expectation of gain in future. Thus foreign exchange market flourished at the cost of more volatility of exchange rates and increasing uncertainties.

The above gives a brief description of the spatial character of money in the perspective of global financial market. How the exchange rate of different currencies move in tandem and what are the important parameters behind this movement will be discussed in Chapter II, which is complementary to the present chapter. Of course the details of the exchange rate mechanism and different theories explaining the movement of the exchange rates will not be discussed in Chapter II as these are covered elsewhere (Nandi, 1996).

The geographical sketch of money and its global character will be taken up in individual details in later chapters of this book where the dynamics of the international flow of money and capital will be presented in both the theoretical and empirical perspectives.

Notes :

1 Embeddedness is a sociological concept which attempts to chart an analytical course between the traditional interpretations of the economic development as explained by the neo-classical economist on the one hand, and Marxism on the other. The concept was first used by Polanyi (1944) for whom the 19th century society was unique in the sense that economic imperatives became dominant in shaping human life. In older societies the economy remained embedded in social relations, subordinated to religious, politics and other social arrangements. Polanyi emphasized that the orientation towards individual economic gains played only a minor role in the primitive societies. But economic self interest became the dominant principle only in the 19th century.

2 The concept of Ricardian equivalence as explained by Barro (1974) implies that an increase in government deficit will induce requisite additional savings from the citizens spontaneously, as the latter realised that extra spending by the government will have to be paid for by taxation in the future. Therefore, additional savings are necessary to meet that eventuality. It is

also shown that, if taxation does not distort the savings behaviour, rational economic agents will buy the extra government debts newly issued to finance the additional expenditure at the same price as it had been prevailing before. This is because the return on this debt instrument will enable the agents to cover the future tax burdens.

One implication of Ricardian equivalence is that in a democratic set up the government is simply an agency to act on behalf of its citizens in the case of borrowing as everything else.

References :

1. Barro R.J., Are government bond net worth ? Journal of Political Economy, 82, 1974, 1095-1117.
2. BIS, Bank for International Settlements 64th Annual Report, 1994, Basle, BIS.
3. BIS, Central bank survey of foreign exchange market activity in April 1992, March 1993, Basle, Bank for International Settlement.
4. Corbridge, S., Maximizing entropy ? New geopolitical orders and the internationalization of business, in Demko G. and W. Wood (eds.), Reordering the World : geopolitical perspectives in the 21st century. Westview, Boulder, Co., 1994.
5. Fleming, J.M., Domestic Financial Policies Under Fixed and Under Floating Exchange Rate, IMF Staff Papers, International Monetary Fund, Vol. 9, 1962, 369-79.
6. Frenkel, J.A. and A. Razin, The Mundell-Fleming Model, A Quarter Century Later : A United Exposition, IMF Staff Papers, 34, 1987, 567-620.
7. Giddens, A. The Nation State and Violence, Cambridge, Polity, 1985.
8. Johns, A., Not tax havens, havens for transnational invisible trade enterprises, Intereconomics, 29 Jan / Feb. 1994, 26-32.
9. Keynes, J.M., The General Theory of Employment, Interest and Money, London, Macmillan, 1936.

10. Lucas, R.E., Studies in the Business Cycle Theory, Cambridge, Mass., M.I.T. Press, 1981.
11. Marx, K., Capital, Vol. 1., Ed. by F. Engels., New York, International, 1867.
12. Massey, D., Power geometry and a progressive sense of place. In J. Bird and other (eds.), Mapping the future-local cultures, global change, Routhedge, London, 1993.
13. Mundell, R. Monetary Theory. Pacific Palisades., Goodyear, 1971.
14. Nandi, S., Essays on International Finance : The Indian Perspective, Pune, National Institute of Bank Management, 1996.
15. O'Brien, R., Global financial integration : The end of geography. London, Pinter, 1991.
16. Polanyi, K., The Great Transformation. Farrarand Reinhart, New York, 1944.
17. Ricardo, D. (1811), The Works and Correspondences of David Ricardo. Vol. III, Pamphlets and Papers, 1809-1811. Edited by P. Srafta, Cambridge, Cambridge University Press, 1951.
18. Thrift, N.J., On the social and cultural determinants of international financial centres : The case of the city of London, in S. Corbridge, R. Martin and N. Thrift (eds.), Money, Power and Space, Oxford, Blackwell, 1994.
19. Zelizer, V.A., The Social Meaning of Money : pin money, paychecks, poor relief, and other currencies. Basic Books, New York, 1994.

II

INTERNATIONAL MONEY AND PAYMENTS

"Money is indeed the most important thing in the world; and all sound and successful personnel and national morality should have this fact for its basis".

J.B. SHAW
The Irrational Knot (1905)
Preface

INTRODUCTION

IN THE THEORY OF EXCHANGE, two agents exchange goods and/or services under the condition that both parties gain through the operation of exchange. In the closed economy set up one agent can procure commodity and/or services in exchange of money, which is the legal tender, and hence acceptable to all. Money is the liability of the central bank of the country, the issuer of the currency. As a legal tender, so long it can be converted into alternative assets, it is universal medium of exchange.

One standard assumption behind the universal acceptance of the domestic legal tender is that the issuer of the currency, i.e. the central bank of the country, will remain committed to maintain stability of the intrinsic value of the currency. In extreme situation when this assumption does not hold or people lose confidence in the sincerity of the central bank, people may not like accepting the currency.

Money as a sovereign legal tender carries the implication that the government will have the backing behind the currency. In many countries the currency also carries the prestige of the ruling authority. The potential implication is that the currency is not acceptable beyond the political boundaries.

In an open economy framework economic agents of two different countries exchange commodities and/or services. Thus the General Motors in the U.S.A. can procure different components of the cars from the Hindustan Motors of India. In such international transactions there should be a system developed enough for the conduct of such international payments system.This requires an international money.

The Bretton Woods System : 1944-1968. Whatever the world coordination system had been existing before the World War II under the agencies of the League of Nations collapsed during the war. At the end of the war, the leaders of the victorious countries felt the urgent need for the establishment of world institutions to take care of the international payments system, which are vital for the world trade and commerce. The thinking of the victorious western nations at that time was dominated by two preoccupations. First, there was urgency in the reconstruction of the economies of Europe and Japan. Second, the countries were eager to prevent a return to the competitive devaluations and protectionism that prevailed in the 1930s. So at Bretton Woods, New Hampshire, the agreement was signed in 1944 and two institutions were born : the International Monetary Fund (IMF) and the International Bank for Reconstruction and Development (IBRD). From the name of the place, the agreement was named as Bretton Woods System.

The objectives of the International Monetary Fund have been to maintain a fixed exchange rate system in the initial period and also to work as the central bank of the central banks of the member countries. In this the member countries undertook two major commitments: (1) to maintain convertibility and (2) to preserve a fixed exchange rate. For the latter the member countries were advised to follow prudent monetary and fiscal policies so that monetary equilibrium in the domestic market was not disturbed. Convertibility of the currency became more a pious intention that a realistic objective as except the U.S.A. none of the member countries was willing to allow free movement of capital in the initial period. Even some years after 1958, the major European currencies offered only current account convertibility. That means that these currencies were freely usable for financing international trade, but were subject to severe restrictions where the purchase or sale of foreign assets were involved.

Regarding the maintenance of the fixed exchange rate regime, the Bretton Woods System became successful. There were few occasions, when changes in the parities (exchange rate of the currencies) were in major scale, and a system of stability in the exchange rate system was seen all through the 1950s and 1960s. During this phase two important events happened. First was the two devaluations of British pound in 1948 and in 1967. The second was the rise of Deutschemark as the German economy recovered and her competitiveness vis-a-vis the U.S.A. increased.Thus Deutschemark emerged as the princi pal currency in Europe.

The world financial system as established in the Bretton Woods Agreement had been established on a principle known as the Gold Exchange Standard, which replaced the 19th Century Gold Standard. In this agreement the U.S.A. remained committed to exchange gold against U.S. dollar at a fixed price, which was $35 per ounce. Thus U.S. dollar was declared international currency. Strictly speaking, the U.S.A. only practised full-fledged Gold Standard and the commitment of dollar-gold parity at a price of $35 per ounce through Gold Window was available to the banks only. Private citizens were not allowed to hold gold in both the U.S.A. and Europe. The important thing is that the requirement of fixing the dollar price of gold are same as fixing the dollar price of other foreign currencies, since the latter were advised to maintain fixed parity with U.S. dollar. Thus the 19th Century Gold Standard was replaced by Gold Exchange Standard through U.S. dollar in the Bretton Woods Agreements.

The Bretton Woods 1968-1973 This period in international finance had been characterised by the following characteristics : the beginning of the deficits in the U. S. current accounts in international trade, the increasing involvement of the U.S.A. in the Vietnam war, the increasing lack of liquidity in the world financial system, the rise of the German Deutschemark and a slow but gradual decline in the demand for U.S. dollars. There were several reasons for all of these and we can put these briefly as follows.

In the beginning when the Treaty was signed in 1944 and the exchange rate parities were fixed, and the dollar gold parity was committed by the U.S.A., the world was dominated by U.S.A. alone, and she controlled virtually total stock of gold. Also her industries enjoyed competitive advantage in terms of efficiency. But as the war ravaged, Europe recovered, and industries began to regain their competitive strength. The relative improvement in productivity situation induced powers which saw the parities of the exchange rates vis-a-vis U.S. dollar not conforming to the reality. Clearly dollar was perceived as over-valued vis-a-vis gold. The perception of the weakness of U.S. dollar is important also in the context of the negative current account of U.S.A. World also saw a surge in inflation leading to sharp increase in the prices of commodities. While prices of commodities had been rising, gold remained under-valued. So a preference for gold developed.

World inflation was reinforced by the decision of the U.S. administration to resort to printing money to cover partly the increasing domestic budget caused by the domestic poverty programme and the Vietnam war. This cheap money policy placed U.S. dollar vis-a-vis deutschemark supported by conservative Bundesbank in a precarious position and dollar was perceived as over-valued. Also the increasing prices of all commodities made the revelation that gold at a price $35 an ounce was a good bargain.

The gold stock of the U.S.A. in comparison to her international obligation (as liability) was seen as inadequate at a gold price of $35 an ounce. The following table reveals this.

Table 1. United States Gold Reserve and Official Liability

Year *(1)*	*Gold Reserve* *(2)*	*Official Liability* *(3)*	*Ratio* *(3:2)*
1960	17.80	21.03	1.18
1961	16.95	22.94	1.35
1962	16.06	24.27	1.51
1963	15.60	26.39	1.69
1964	15.47	29.36	1.90
1965	14.07	29.57	2.10
1966	13.24	31.02	2.34
1967	12.07	36.67	2.96
1968	10.89	38.47	3.53
1969	11.86	45.91	3.86
1970	11.07	46.96	4.24
1971	11.08	67.81	6.12

Source : IMF : International Financial Statistics

International politics also came to the picture as the Gaullist French administration started large scale substitution of dollar by gold in her international reserve. This led to an excess supply of U.S. dollar.

Given the above perspective whatever was warranted happened. To prevent the outflow of gold from the United States, President Nixon announced the closing of Gold Window on August 15, 1971. With this the Bretton Woods System collapsed.

An attempt was made to save the system through Smithsonian agreement in which gold was priced as \$38 an ounce from the old level of \$35. But this did not become effective, and broke down after one year.

Before the collapse of the Bretton Woods System, the very basis of the fixed exchange rate system had been debated in the economics profession. A relatively small but powerful section of the profession favoured a flexible exchange rate system instead of the fixed rate one. They argued that the disequilibrium in the domestic money market in the form of mismatch between the aggregate demand for and the supply of money should be allowed to be corrected through its spill over in the external sector of the economy in the changes of both balance of payments and exchange rate. Instead of periodic changes, exchange rate should remain flexible, and this helps in keeping the domestic prices in their true position. But the structure of the Bretton Woods System could not adjust to the flexible exchange rate system due to the gold-dollar parity as committed by the U.S.A. government.

The Floating Rate Era : 1973 onwards. This period of floating rates experienced a relatively high volatility of the exchange rates. U.S. dollar surged ahead against all major currencies till 1984 and then the intervention of G-10 countries helped the sliding down of the dollar. The period also witnessed two quick shocks of the excessive hike of the petroleum prices in

1973 and 1977 and that induced the inflation in the world and changed the terms of trade of the petroleum importing countries. The major characteristics of this period can be put in order.

The U.S.A. experienced a large current account deficit, which touched $100 billion in 1990 with a very low saving-income ratio at the domestic level. On the other hand Germany and Japan experienced large current account surplus, which are largely with the U.S.A.

There has been a global insolvency problem as a large number of countries became unable to service their debt. The petro dollars in the initial period were recycled by the international banks to the needy third world countries at high nominal interest rates. Subsequently inflation came down, but not the interest rate. This led to a substantial rise in real interest rate and a higher debt burden on the developing countries.

There has been a definite change in the balance of economic power in the world with the rise of Japan and Germany as economic power houses. Particularly, Japan supplied capital to a large number of countries including the USA. On the other hand Germany alongwith European Union became a significant economic force to reckon with.

The world has also seen huge amount of trans-border capital flow and this has been helped by technological innovation. There has been a phenomenal increase in the volume of business of international forex market and international market of derivatives. In 1997 the average daily transaction of international forex market reached $1.6 trillion approximately.

Along with the increase in the business there has been a perceptible increase in the volatility in the market. This is the result of increasing uncertainty about the perception of the market operations. Again this increasing risk factor has induced development in the derivative market.

On November 1, 1993 the Maastricht Treaty came into force

and created the European Union. By the end of 1997, 11 members of EU fulfilled the criteria for the launch of the common currency EURO from January 1, 1999. When Euro will replace the currencies of the members on July 1, 2002 (the period between January 1 and June 30, 2002 will see a dual currency system as Euro will come into circulation along with national currencies), it will be the currency of one of the largest economic block of the world. Then its relation with U.S. dollar will be worthy of watching. Many economists are exploring now to what extent Euro will replace U.S. dollar in the total international reserve of the member states.

The floating exchange rate regime since 1973 ultimately became unsatisfactory and in the international level this was mainly for three reasons. First, inflation had been common world phenomenon and there was hardly any uniformity regarding this in member countries. This was because of divergent macroeconomic policies followed by the members.

Second, the world economy was subject to two severe shocks, the OPEC oil price hike in 1973 and 1979. It was difficult for any exchange rate mechanism to absorb this shock. It reinforced inflation in the oil importing countries and altered the terms of trade.

Third, international financial system was being dominated by rising tide of international capital flows. That started creating uncertainty and the exchange rate volatility increased.

In the international diplomacy the U.S.A. on the one side and Europe and Japan on the other were advancing disparate arguments for the stability of the exchange rate system. While U.S.A. was arguing that Japan and Europe should adopt expansionist policies so that U.S.A. could increase exports and cut down deficits in current accounts, Japan argued that U.S.A. should take measures to reduce budget deficits, as the latter was the root cause of the current account deficit.

In September 1985 the Finance Ministers of G-7 countries

met at Plaza Hotel in New York and reached an agreement that U.S. dollar should be allowed to fall. They agreed a target zone for U.S. dollar. In February, 1987 the ministers of G-7 met again, but this time at Louvre in Paris and agreed that the fall of U.S. dollar had been adequate and should be stabilised.

Since the Plaza-Louvre accord central banks in G-7 countries have conducted concerted intervention several times for the stabilisation of dollar and they had been successful. On certain occasions central banks of three countries, i.e., the U.S.A., Japan and Germany, intervened in unison and had been able to achieve the targets.

The relationship between IMF and the G-7 countries (the U.S.A., Canada, France, Germany, Italy, Japan, the United Kingdom) is unique in the sense that these countries have a long history of meeting on the economic and financial matters of common concern for a long time atleast since 1970. The arrangement was formalised at the 1982 Versailles Summit of the G-7, where these seven countries declared their eagerness to strengthen their cooperation with the IMF in its work of surveillance. During the period 1981 to 1985 the U.S.A. followed a policy of "being neglect" regarding the exchange rate of dollar and G-7 countries could do little on this. It is only after 1985 Plaza Meeting the G-7 countries became active for the stabilisation of the exchange rate regime. Since that time these countries are active for the management of the world exchange rate system.

The power the G-7 countries exercise in the management of the world financial system is derived from the voting power within the IMF. These countries control about 47 per cent of the votes in the Board of Governors of the IMF and slightly over 50 per cent in the Executive Board. In the latter the Canadian and Italian directors exercise the votes of all countries that have elected them and where the voting power of a few new members is not exercised.

The Prices In An Open Economy In any economic system taxation and subsidies, the most powerful tools in the hands of the government, create distortion in the system of prices, and the economists thus remain satisfied with the second best solution. But assuming that no tax is there the price of a commodity should reflect the true opportunity cost, both from the producer's side and from the consumer's side. This also leads to the Law of One Price which states :

If two goods are identical, they must sell for the same price.

The implication of the above statement is that if the statement does not hold, some people will take advantage out of that to make money. This process is known as arbitrage, which is defined as :

Arbitrage is an action of buying or selling some commodity in order to exploit a price differential so as to make a profit.

Over time the Law of One price holds through the actions of arbitrage by the economic agents. That is true for the international transactions of commodities also. Both India and Sri Lanka are the exporters of tea. If the two quotations in the international market are different for the same quality of tea, some traders will resort to arbitrage operations to make a profit. What is true for tea is true for all types of commodities. This is one area where market forces act precisely like the law of physics.

One should be cautious about the difference between the arbitrage and speculation. Speculation is defined as activity of holding a good in the hope of profiting from a future rise in prices. The core of the speculation is having or creating a stake on the uncertainty about the future. Thus in a market one finds three categories of economic agents : the traders, the arbitrageurs and the speculators. In reality though sometimes actions of these three classes overlap, or the same person may perform multiple roles.

EXCHANGE RATES In international market, currency is traded like a commodity. Why is the currency of a foreign country needed?

The answer is that if an Indian trader wants to buy colour picture tubes from Japan, the seller of Japan is to be paid in Japanese yen. Now the Indian trader is to convert rupees into yen by paying the latter in the foreign exchange market, which should be properly called as foreign currency market. The price of yen is known as exchange rate. The definition is :

The exchange rate of a currency, say Indian rupee, is the rupee value of foreign currency, say U.S. dollar.

Thus we quote U.S. $ 1 = Rs. 43.00, we simply say that Rs. 43.00 is to be paid to have one U.S. dollar.

All exchange rates quotation comes as a two-way quotes, or bid-offer rates. The bid rate for U.S. dollar in terms of rupee is the rate at which dealers buy dollar and sell rupees. Again, the offer rate or ask rate is the rate at which the dealer sell dollars and buy rupees. Also the bid/ask spread is the gap between the offer rate and bid rates and the extent of this spread reveals both the depth of the market and the volatility of the exchange rate in some situations.

Exchange rate information comes either as spot rate or as forward rate. The spot rate is relevant for current transaction, i.e. the exchange of the two currencies take place at the present time, though in the international market spot delivery can stretch upto 48 hours.

The forward rate is the price of a currency in terms of the

domestic currency when the delivery will take place along with the payments at some future date, say after 90 days or 180 days. It is a future contract between two parties.

The Relation Between Spot And Forward Rates

Like any commodity the present and future prices of a currency differ, but unlike the ordinary commodity prices, here the two prices are linked up precisely by the important economic parameter, and that is the interest rate. To reach that conclusion two concepts require explanation–the uncovered interest rate parity condition, and covered interest rate parity condition.

The uncovered interest rate parity condition (UIRP) states that the domestic interest rate must be higher than the foreign interest rate by an amount equal to the expected depreciation of the domestic currency, or where x is the expected depreciation of the domestic currency, i the domestic interest rate and i^* the foreign rate. When the domestic currency is stronger, domestic interest rate becomes less than foreign rate and the domestic currency appreciates.

The UIRP condition is also known in international finance literature in another name, or the international Fisher Equation. The implication is that the domestic nominal interest rate should compensate adequately depreciation of the domestic currency. When this is not the case, flight from the domestic currency takes place, which is nothing but capital flights from the economy.

The covered interest parity condition (CIP) states that the domestic interest rate must be higher than the foreign interest rate by an amount equal to the forward discount on the domestic currency. We can write this in equation form as :

$$i = i^* + x$$

$$(1 + i) = (1 + i_*). \frac{F}{S}, \qquad \text{.......... (2) or}$$

$$F = \frac{S(1 + i)}{(1 + i^*)} \qquad \text{.......... (3) or}$$

$$F = \frac{S+S(i - i^*)}{(i + i^*)} \qquad \text{.......... (4)}$$

Equations (2), (3) and (4) are equivalent expression. Here F and S stand for forward rate and spot rate respectively for the domestic currency. Using the direct quote norm, it is clear from equation (4) that when the domestic interest rate rises and becomes higher than the foreign interest rate, the second term on the right determines the premium for the foreign currency, which is equivalent to saying that domestic currency is sold at a discount, the latter is determined by the interest differential.

Equation (4) also guides the market arbitrage conditions, as the participants always monitor the movement of the domestic interest rate i vis-a-vis the foreign rate i*. Whenever the market values gives inequality in equation (4), perfect arbitrage dictates sale or purchase of the currency to take advantage of the interest differential. Thus the market forces restores the equality again, which is the equilibrium situation of the market.

There is a hypothesis which states that forward rate is the unbiased predictor of the future spot rate. There has been scores of paper empirically testing the relationship between the two rates.

Some recent results are worth mentioning:

For the period May 1980 to March 1990, the monthly data of Japanese yen were used to estimate the econometric equation as

Spot (t) = $a^o + a^1$ Forward rate (t-1) + error

The estimation gives the result like

	S^t =	-0.0057 + 1.0005 F t-1 +e
t-value		(-0.0019) (69.94)

R_{-2} = 0.978
SER = 7.248
n = 110

For deutschemark and in the same period covering, the estimation results is like.

	S^t =	$0.0278 + 0.99 F^{t-1} + e$
t-value		(0.6398) (53.38)

R_{-2} = 0.963
SER = 0.084
n = 110

Clearly both the results show that intercept term is not significant and one period lag value of forward rate determines the spot rate with high degree of accuracy. This econometric result helps to have an understanding of where the rate is going in the immediate future.

The participants' conjecture about the potential price movement are conditional on the assumption of full information set. This is possible in an efficient market.

Efficient Market Hypothesis The concept of market efficiency was first developed in the finance literature and its full form was explained by Eugene Fama. But nowadays this concept is being used in other areas also. Efficient market is defined as the one where prices fully reflect all the available information. By definition then there should not exist any unexplained opportunities for profit.

The definition of efficient market is a little vague and its vagueness is, it seems, intentional. It can be shown that, under certain circumstances, it is not required that all market operators to share exactly identical view of the future price. Some investors may be better informed than the rest.

The implication of the concept of market efficiency in forex market is interesting. Let us assume that both spot and forward markets of a currency are characterised by the following conditions:

(a) There are a large number of investors with ample funds available for arbitrage operations, and

(b) There is no exchange control and also no transaction cost.

In this situation suppose an American investor thinks that spot price of deutschemark (DM) in terms of dollars is going to be 15 per cent higher in 12 months than it is today. The investor may be able to profit by buying DM forward, and then selling DM spot at the end of 12 months. If he proves right in his judgement, his profit will be 15 per cent less the premium paid for forward DM (transaction cost is nil as assumed). As the market information is perfect, other investors will follow suit, and the forward DM will be bid up until the premium is high enough to prevent any further speculation.

One interesting question is how long the participants indulge in speculation in the market to have a share of the profit. This is not indefinite, as at some point investors will realise that, although the potential of profit from speculation is not zero, the probable reward is not great enough to compensate for the risk of being wrong. Thus equilibrium will be reached and speculation will stop at the point, where the gap between the forward rate and the expectation of the market of the future spot rate is just equal to the required risk premium charged, or in equation it becomes $f^t(t-1) = E^t\,(S^{t}+1) + r^t$ where LHS is the logarithm of forward price of DM at time t for delivery at period (t-1) and r^t is the risk premium. In the above equation the forward rate reflects both the publicly available information congealed in the rational expectation $E^t(S^t+1)$ and the attitude of the market towards risk revealed in the risk premium. Thus the equation shows the equilibrium in the efficient market. The interpretation of efficiency explained here corresponds to what E. Fama called semi-strong form of efficiency (Fame, 1970). Strong form of efficiency applies when the market price reflects all information, whether publicly available or not.

It is quite possible to image a situation where the market price reflects only the restricted information set which can be used in the formation of weak rational expectations. Here the expected value in the equation would be conditioned on the past value of the time series, and not on the universe of publicly available information. This helps defining a weak efficient market.

A weak efficient market is one where the market price reflects the information in its own past history. It implies that there no longer exists any opportunity to profit by making use of past time series of prices alone.

One interesting aspect of weak efficient market is that the latter will normally offer opportunities to make a profit by the exploitation of information additional to the past time series to prices. Another implication of market efficiency is the unbiasedness of the market.

A forex market is said to be unbiased when the forward market is efficient and investors are risk neutral, so that the forward rate is equal to the mathematical expectation of the spot rate at the time of the maturation of the contract.

Efficient or inefficient players in the forex market are big and they are equipped with very powerful computers with famous softwares. Inspite of the fact that they have access to massive data set and powerful software, calculations go wrong and survey data repeatedly point out irrational movement of expectation. May be this is another mystery of the market forces.

Global payments system and mobility of money The world is much more integrated today and commodities and money move across the countries at a speed much faster compared to even 40 or 50 years ago. While the theory of international trade explains the framework of the movement of commodities across the countries, international finance gives the theoretical framework of the movement of money and capital across the political boundaries. The exchange rate mechanism explains the analytical framework of how the international payments are made. Thus an Indian firm can buy cotton from an Egyptian company through a transaction process made through the banking system and some government organisation. But the same channel facilitates the movement of money which may not be directly related to trade.

Let us consider the three types of agents in the economy–the individual, the firm and the government. Suppose the government desires an accelerated rate of economic growth for which a higher rate of investment is required. If the domestic savings are not adequate to match this investment, the government can encourage inflow of foreign capital. This capital inflow may assume different forms : grants or loan at the government-to-government level, private capital inflow into the equities of the domestic industries, or foreign direct investment. Regardless of the form of the capital inflow, this bridges the gap between the domestic savings and investment. The nature of capital mobility in the process has been discussed in Chapter III. One interesting hypothesis discussed in the chapter is that in the context of perfect capital mobility at the international level, domestic saving and investment are not correlated.

One particular form of capital mobility across the boundaries of the nations is the flight of capital to other countries through the means not sanctioned by the legal system of the country. This is known as capital flight in the literature. The basic idea is that every rational economic agent will try to maintain the intrinsic value of the savings. When this remains no longer guaranteed because of the faulty taxation system and/or high inflationary situation, capital flight takes place and it goes to a safe destination (Boyce, 1992).This aspect has been analysed in detail in Chapter IV.

Money is an institution characterised by the legal system of the country. Except a few countries, citizens of the country are not allowed to hold foreign exchange and to deal with foreign exchange. Transaction at the international level is done through the central bank. For this the latter is to maintain a reserve consisting of foreign currencies, special drawing rights (SDR) and gold. This international reserve of the central bank is the provider of liquidity to the country's transactions with the outside world. The country is to maintain an optimum dose of liquidity, and that determines the adequacy of the level of international reserve. This is also important to keep the stability of the exchange rate of domestic currency. This topic has been discussed in Chapter V. One important lesson of the crisis of the currency melt down of South Asian countries is that the countries could not maintain adequate level of international measure to provide liquidity to the firms engaged in international transactions.

References :

Boyce, J. K., The Revolving Door? External Debt and Capital Flight : A Philippine Case Study, World Development 20(3), March, 1992, 335-349.

Fama,.E.F., Efficient Capital Markets : A Review of Theory and Empirical Evidence, Journal of Finance, 25, 1970, 383-417.

III

INTERNATIONAL CAPITAL MOBILITY :

INTRODUCTION

International Mobility Of Factors of production, including capital but excluding human labour, is being encouraged through the recently concluded multi-country trade agreements.

First in the industrialised countries, and then in some of the advanced developing countries capital markets are seen to be highly correlated through the transactions of funds across political boundaries. The dawn of the 20th century experienced the integration of the world commodity markets. The period after the World War II saw an unprecedented expansion of international trade in merchandise. To cater to the needs of the latter, the scope of international banking expanded in the 60s and 70s. Meanwhile countries were convinced about the positive aspects of international trade. One lesson of the latter is that the root of the competitiveness lies in cost reduction and labour is one important factor in the latter. Now international companies started the practice of establishing the production unit near the markets. This has at least two advantages. First, it reduces the transport cost to a large extent, especially for the commodities which are of the weight gaining character. Thus Japanese car companies have established their production units in the U.S.A. to supply cars in the U.S.A.'s domestic market. Of course, long before this, capital moved to foreign countries to "manufacture" services. Thus British banks in India or Indian traders in some countries of Africa were seen in the 19th century itself.

Second, by shifting the production base, the multinational companies can get labour at much cheaper rate compared to domestic markets. Thus the U.S. companies shifted their base of production or assembly line in the developing countries like Taiwan or Hong Kong long ago.

In both the cases, capital had been invested in the foreign countries through equity participation. The host countries were benefited in more than one way apart from the direct benefits of employment.

The mobility of capital across the political boundaries has other implications. The microeconomic theories teach us that the capital formation of a country depends on her overall savings. In fact, steady-state growth of a closed economy is said to depend on the saving-income ratio and the incremental capital-output ratio. This induces the economists to prescribe for higher rate of savings which will guarantee a higher rate of capital formation.

The question which is important is that whether a country with low saving-income ratio can expect higher rate of growth depending on the borrowed funds, by encouraging direct foreign investments. To put the issue in a different perspective, it boils down to the question to what extent capital is mobile across the political boundaries. If the capital mobility is high, a country with a lower saving-income ratio can afford higher investment depending on foreign capital. This implies that saving-income ratio (S/Y ratio) and investment-income ratio (I/Y ratio) may be independent. The degree of independence of these two ratios and the degree of capital mobility are analytically related.

Theories of International Capital Mobility The study of the international capital mobility and the financial integration of the capital markets of different countries tries to trace the common elements affecting both. The literature also defines weak and strong form of financial integration. A weak form of financial integration refers to a situation when domestic and foreign economic agents trade identical assets at the same price. This implies that law of one price prevails in the absence of artificial barriers. But foreign assets may be imperfect substitutes because of different political regimes. But financial integration is said to be strong when identically defined assets denominated in different currencies under different political regimes are perfect substitutes to the economic agents.

Economies that have experienced some kind of financial integration already and also the countries which are trying to integrate their capital market with the international capital market should be cautious of some implications of the financial integration (Montiel, 1994). Assuming that all domestic interest bearing assets are perfect substitutes, first it can be said that changes in excess supplies and demands of assets in a small economy have no influence on the world prices of the assets. When the latter rule in the domestic market, returns on assets become less sensitive to the changes in domestic saving schedule.

As for example, even if real return on savings goes down, capital can be shifted abroad to realise the expected return.

Second, one implication of the open economy macroeconomics literature is that the effects of domestic fiscal and monetary policies on aggregate demand depends on the degree of financial integration of the economy with the outside world. As for example, under the fixed exchange rate regime, strong financial integration implies that neither fiscal nor monetary policies can influence the conditions of domestic borrowing.

Third, when the degree of integration of an economy increases, the effects of a given fiscal deficit on inflation increase for the following reasons. The latter depends on two things : the stock of base money and the elasticity of base money demand with respect to rate of inflation. As the degree of integration increases, less the economic agents can increasingly dodge the inflation tax by a suitable change of their portfolios. Thus the scope of the inflation tax is reduced and increasing impact of the fiscal deficit is felt on the price level. This aspect is important for the developing economies which are increasingly seeking integration with the international capital market.

Theoretically, the issue of financial integration on international capital mobility has been approached form a variety of angles. Many economists have tried to measure the extent of gross or net capital flows among the countries. Based mainly on the industrial countries various measures are obtained in Golub (1990), Feldstein (1986), Capino and Howard (1984), Obstfeld (1986) and Penati and Dooky (1984). Also many major developing countries have experienced huge outflow of capital through their financial openness (Cuddington, 1986; Montiel, 1993).

When a country is highly integrated with rest of the world, it is expected that country will experience a high level of capital flows. Generally, two reasons are cited in the literature (Montiel, 1994). First, in a strong integrated market borrowing and lending can often cross political boundaries. The present day Europe is an example. Second, in case of financial integration, the term structure of interest rates at the domestic level is related to the level of the world and any change on either side in the rates of return will induce net capital inflow. The latter helps in the equalisation of the returns which is generally measured by covered interest parity, uncovered interest parity and real interest parity. Again, for most developing countries covered interest parity is of little empirical relevance because, for the currencies of such countries, forward markets seldom exist.

For the developing countries uncovered interest parity (UIP) is most relevant and it states that arbitrage equalizes expected returns on same type of foreign and domestic assets, or

$$(1 + i_t) = E[(1+i^*_t)\, S_{t+1}/S_t] \qquad \text{......1}$$

Where i_t is domestic and i^* foreign interest rate and S_t is the domestic currency price of one unit of foreign currency. Here both i_t and S_{t+1} are stochastic variables because of the risk factor. Since RHS of equation (1) is not observable, we use rational expectation hypothesis (REH). Under the assumption of REH,.ls

$$(1+i^*_t)\, S_{t+1}/S_t = E[(1+i^*_t)\, S_{t+1}/S_t] + e \qquad \text{......2}$$

Where e is the prediction error, a random variable with zero mean. When the market is weakly efficient, the information set should contain the past prediction error, which is the lagged value of e_t, and this is serially uncorrelated. We consider the expost differential d_t, given by

$$d_t = (1 + i_t) - (1 + i^*_t)\, S_{t+1}/S_t \qquad \text{.....3}$$

Under the null hypothesis of UIP and rational expectation, d_t is the negative prediction error.

Thus the joint hypothesis can be tested by examining whether d_t has a zero mean and is not serially correlated.

One implication of the testing of the UIP is that the difference between the prices of identical assets in two countries shows the degree of financial integration. As the latter increases, the difference gets narrower.

Another aspect of financial integration is that as capital inflow is influenced by the differences in real returns, the changes in the savings levels of a country should have little bearing on the investment. In a more formal level, Feldstein and Horioka (1980) defined perfect capital mobility in the sense that exogenous changes in the national savings rate should have no effects on the investment rate.

The Feldstein-Horioka (F-H) condition requires that the real interest rate of the country should be tied with the same of the world by real interest parity condition. Further, it is also necessary that all determinants of a country's rate of investment other than its real interest rate be uncorrelated with its rate of national saving.

The estimable regression in the F-H approach is

$$(I/Y)_t = a + b\,(S/Y)_t + e$$

where (I/Y) is the ratio of gross domestic investment to gross national product (GNP), and (S/Y) is the ratio of national savings to GNP. The argument is that under the hypothesis of perfect capital mobility, b should be zero for small countries. Again, for large countries, b should approximate the country's share of the world capital stock.

The original estimate of b in F-H study was close to 0.9 and they interpreted that value as consistent with a low degree of financial integration. This observation based on the high value of b is challenged by many economists, though the findings of F-H for large industrial countries have been confirmed in many studies. Further, in some estimates the estimated value of 'b' has been statistically different from the auturky value 1 indicating some degree of financial integration. We will get more scope for the discussion of F-H condition later.

It is stated above that the F-H condition requires that real interest parity should hold, or

$$r_i - r^* = 0$$

where r^* is the world interest rate and is exogenous. One criticism (Tobin, 1983; Murphy, 1984) is that if domestic country is large in the international market, r^* will not be exogenous, and therefore, even if

$$r_i - r^* = 0$$

r and in turn (I/Y) will be correlated with (S/Y). It means that a decrease in the domestic savings will drive up world interest rate and thus crowd out investment both in the domestic economy and also abroad.

Further, if saving-investment regression is a good test for financial integration, the coefficient 'b' is expected to fall over time. But evidence does not support this either in cross-section studies (Feldstein, 1983; Dooley et al, 1987) or in time-series study (Frankel, 1986; Obstfeld, 1986). Often endogeneity of the national savings is mentioned for this result, but opinion differs, as use of an instrumental variable does not change the result (Frankel, 1992).

Sometimes it is assumed that the domestic market clearing interest rate (say i') can be expressed as a weighted average of the uncovered interest parity interest rate (i^*) and the domestic market clearing interest rate that would be observed in the case of complete closed (say i'). Edwards and Khan (1985) made such an assumption and formally it means

$$i = w\, i^* + (1 - w)\, i' \qquad \text{.......(1)}$$

when 0 _ w _ 1

Here the estimated value of the parameter w is supposed to reveal the structural feature of the economy. When $w = 1$, we have perfect capital mobility as the domestic market clearing interest rate equals the uncovered interest parity.

A slight regrouping of the equation (1) gives

$$i - i^{*} = (1 - w)(i' - i^{*}) \qquad \text{...... (2)}$$

or this implies that deviations from uncovered parity are proportional to the divergence between the interest rate corresponding to the closed private capital account and the uncovered parity (external) rate. This type of situation may emerge when capital controls are partially relaxed (Haque and Montiel, 1991).

To derive an expression for the complete closed economy interest rate i, Haque and Montiel (1991) starts with the money supply identity.

$$M = R + D \qquad \text{......(3)}$$

when M = domestic money supply

R = domestic currency value of foreign exchange reserve, and

D = stock of domestic credit outstanding

$$\text{Also, } M_t = R_{t-1} + D_t + d(R) \qquad \text{......(4)}$$

where d(R) denotes the change in the domestic value of foreign exchange reserve in period t. Using the balance of payment identity we can write,

$$d(R) = CA + KA^G + KA^D \qquad \text{......(5)}$$

Where CA, KA^G, KA^D are the surplus (or deficit) of the domestic currency value of current account, public capital account and private capital account respectively. So equation (4) can be written as

$$M^t = R^{t-1} + D + CA + KA^G + KA^D \qquad \text{......(6)}$$

Again, when private capital account is completely closed, the revised money supply equation stands as (omitting the term KA^D and denoting this money supply as M'),

$$M' = R^{t-1} + D + CA + KA^G, \text{ and}$$
$$M' = M - KA^D \qquad ....(7)$$

Taking the conventional form of the demand for money equation

$$\log (M/P)_t = a_o + a_1 i + a_2 \log y + a_3 \log (M/P)_{t-1}$$

$$\text{with } a_1 < O, a_2 > O, a_3 > O \qquad ......(8)$$

Where y is real output and P is the domestic price level. (Also M is not used in equation (8) as current demand depends on the actual money stock in previous period rather than the hypothetical money stock corresponding to the zero capital mobility in private account). Again the interest rate i' is that value of i which emerges out of the equilibrium in the money market or imposing equilibrium condition.

$$\log (M' / P) = \log (M^d / P) \text{ and}$$

from equation (8) we have $i' = (a_0 / a_1) + (1/a_1) \log (M/P) - (a_2/a_1) \log y - (a_3/a_1) \log (M/P)_{t-1}$ ......(9)

Since most of the developing countries experience financial repression, the data on market clearing interest rate are not available. To solve this problem. Haque and Motiel (1991) has proceeded in two stages. First, equation (9) is substituted in equation (1) to get an expression for the unobserved variable i. In this stage two the resulting expression is substituted in equation (8) and then both equation (8) and equation (6) are substituted in equation (8), which is the equilibrium condition and the following expression is obtained,

$$\log (M/P) = b_0 + b_1 i + b_2 \log (M/P) + b_3 \log y + b_4 \log (M/P)^{t-1} \qquad .....(10)$$

with $b_0 = a_0 (1 - w)$

$b_1 = a_1 w < 0$

$b_2 = 1 - w \;:\; 0 <= b^2 \_ 1$

$b_3 = a_2 w > 0$

$b_4 = a_3 w > 0$

all variables in equation (10) are observable and estimation of it by non-linear instrumental variables method will result in the estimates of the parameters, particularly of the money demand parameters given by a's and capital mobility parameter w. The estimated value of w, which has been obtained as a positive fraction, shows different degree of capital mobility in the sample countries.

Different aspects of capital mobility have also been studied in the literature. Some of the important aspects are : the relevance of monetary autonomy (Takagi, 1986, the interest differential as a result of capital control (Phylaktis, 1988) and the hypothesis of perfect capital mobility in the context of a macroeconometric model (Haque, Lahiri and Montiel, 1990). The last one has used a general equilibrium approach for the estimation of a simultaneous equation system based on Indian data.

3. Capital Mobility: Saving-Investment Relation

The model of Feldstein and Horioka (1980) has been explained in the earlier chapter. The equation for estimation is

$$(I/Y) = a + b\,(S/Y) + e \qquad ......\ (3.1)$$

where (I/Y) is the ratio of gross domestic investment to gross national product, and (S/Y) is the ratio of domestic saving to GNP. The authors argue that under the null hypothesis of perfect capital mobility, b should be zero for small countries.

Again, for large countries b should approximate the value of the parameters which reveals the country's share of the world capital stock. This approach based on the correlation between saving and investment suffers from the conceptual problem of the following kind (Montiel, 1994) : Zero capital mobility implies that I/Y and S/Y would be highly correlated, but the converse is not true. i.e., even if world financial markets are perfectly integrated, saving and investment rates could be highly correlated. Two explanations are offered for this. First, two ratios (I/Y) and (S/Y) may be correlated even if real interest parity also holds, because both of them are endogenous variables responding to the movement of a third economic factor. One example is that both the ratios could be functions of the state of the business cycles.

Second, since goods markets are not well integrated compared to the financial market, even under uncovered interest parity, shocks that are specific to savings or investment could also lead to a positive correlation between the two variables (Frankel, 1986, 1992).

Feldstein-Horioka Equation : Cross-section result :

The F-H equation

$$I/Y = a + b\,(S/Y) + e$$

has been estimated with cross-section data of 30 countries for two different years, 1990 and 1993. The names of the countries are given in Table 1.

the result for the year 1990 is

I/Y = 0.1602 + 0.3079 (S/Y) + e

t-value (5.246) (2.57)

Adjusted R^2 = 0.162 n = 30

D.W. statistic = 1.134

S.E.E. = 0.097

The result for the year 1993 is

I/Y = -0.0139 + 1.177 (S/Y)

t-value (-0.174) (44.29)

Adjusted R^2 = 0.985

D.W. statistic = 2.96

S.E.E. = 4.33

The cross-section results show that for the year 1990 the estimated value of b is 0.308, which is much less than unity. This shows a fair degree of financial integration, though this is significantly different from zero, the result of the year 1993 is interesting, which shows the estimated value of b as 1.177, and this significantly higher than unity. We can remember our earlier caution that a very high value of b close to 1 does not necessarily mean that capital mobility at the international level is zero.

The same data set has been used to see whether cross-section wise the investment/GDP ratio has any relation with the lending rate of the countries (a good proxy for the interest rate). In both the years, the regression are not significant. Thus for the year 1990 the estimated regression is

I/Y = 0.2366 - 0.0000912 LR

t-ratio (18.807) (0.677)

Adjusted R^2 = -0.019

DW statistic = 1.08

SEE = 0.118

Table 1
The names of the 30 countries in the cross-section regression

India	Fiji	Hungary
Pakistan	U.S.A.	Sweden
Sri Lanka	Canada	Australia
Bangladesh	Mexico	New Zealand
Singapore	Venezuela	Czechoslovakia
Indonesia	Poland	Austria
Malaysia	United Kingdom	France
Korea	Germany	Greece
Phili ppines	Switzerland	Italy
Thailand	Spain	Cyprus

The empirical estimation of the Feldstein-Horioka equation has been done on the basis of time series of some countries. The results are given in Table 2. In this time-series regression 25 countries are taken as their names appear.The period of the study for all these countries is, in general, 1960 to 1989. To tackle serial correlation, Cochrane-Orcutt method of estimation has been done. All data are taken from International Financial Statistics (IMF). According to Feldstein-Horioka (1980) study for the null hypothesis of perfect financial integration (or capital mobility), b = o or the estimated value of b will not be significantly different from zero. A very weak financial integration should lead to the estimated value of 'b' close to 1.

From the Table 2 we see that in 10 cases the estimated coefficient 'b' is not significantly different from zero, or in the case of these countries, financial integration is very close. The countries are: Venezuela, Japan, Netherlands, Sri Lanka, Thailand, Zambia, Nigeria, Ghana and Pakistan. While one would not like to see the name of Japan in this group, perhaps the huge savings generated by Japan finds its place of investment elsewhere in the form of huge trade surplus the country has been enjoying for a long time. One difficulty of the empirical test of the Feldstein-Horioka condition is that a single test often may not be enough to make judgement about the aggregate macroeconomic phenomenon of a country as the latter is much more a complex phenomenon compared to the correlation of the two important ratios–the saving–GDP ratio and the investment GDP ratio.

In two cases (Greece and Italy), the estimated value of b is higher than 1, though in both cases the estimated values are significantly different from 1 at 5 per cent level of significance (the t values for the t - test are 1.55 and 1.356 respectively).

In 13 other cases the estimated values of 'b' are positive fraction and significantly different from zero. The value of b ranges from 0.99 for Austria to 0.207 for India. The latter figure is significant at 7.8 per cent level of significance. This result is interesting, because India's planned economy and a rigid control regime signify a low mobility of capital, and hence a high value of b. Perhaps the caution that a very low value of b does not necessarily imply higher level of financial integration is more meaningful in the case of India. Another important aspect of the empirical result is that in most of the cases the value of adjusted R^2 is quite high. Of course, in two cases, Chile and Thailand, R^2 is very poor and regressions are not meaningful. Further, in cases of Zambia (0.338), Italy (0.52) and Pakistan (0.47), the value of adjusted R^2 is not high. We are to remember that in all cases the problem of serial correlation in time-series data has been taken care of with the use of Cochrane-Orcutt method of estimation.

Thus the overall results show that the estimated values of b do not support the higher level of financial integration of the world. This vindicates the contention of Feldstein-Horioka. Also the time-series study on the basis of data of 25 countries shows the financial integration of the world, capital mobility is far from perfect (or the value of b is significantly different from zero). This is quite consistent with the result of cross-section study reported in the beginning of this chapter.

The results as explained above in both cross-section and time-series cases are robust and one interpretation of the same may be that there are significant bottlenecks in the international capital markets for the smooth mobility of capital. This aspect of the international capital market requires more serious attention.

A Critique Of Feldstein-Horioka Correlation A recent study (Sinn, 1992) has evaluated the use of saving-investment correlation to measure the mobility of capital. It has been argued that the intertemporal approach to the balance of payments predicts that the estimation of the correlation between saving and investment shares in GDP from long term data creates a bias in favour of accepting the hypothesis of capital mobility. But the new evidence put forward in the paper (Sinn, 1992) does not overturn Feldstein and Horioka's findings of high correlation between saving and investment. Further, this high correlation has been accepted in the literature as a robust empirical regularity. A very good summary is available in Wong (1990) and Frankel (1991).

The high correlation between saving and investment has been seen from various angles. e.g., cyclical movement of national income can produce the high relation (Obstfeld, 1986), or the presence of non-traded consumption good (Murphy, 1986; Wong, 1990). Sometimes economists have analysed the high correlation as the result of government actions, that is, government can offset private net capital flow by suitable policies to prevent large current account balances (Tobin, 1983; Westphal, 1983: Summers, 1988 and Bayoumi, 1990).

There is also one country size argument (Harberger, 1980) which argues that for a large country, the need to borrow from abroad to face any economic shock is not so high as it can diversify its needs. Most of the countries included in the study of Feldstein and Horioka (1980) are large. But subsequent study like Feldstein and Bacchetta (1991) has also supported the original F-H hypothesis.

Table 2

Time-Series Regression : (I/Y) = a + b (S/Y) + e

Sr. No.	Country/ period	a	b	adjusted R^2	D.W.	SEE
1.	India (1960-88)	18.05 (6.34)	0.207 (1.894)	0.79	1.95	41.52
2.	Korea (1960-89)	16.497 (5.85)	0.472 (4.23)	0.82	1.678	179.77
3.	Malaysia (1960-89)	33.0 (3.55)	-0.112 (-0.77)	0.84	1.416	200.6
4.	Chile (1960-89)	10.39 (3.87)	0.33 (2.06)	0.134	1.88	366.7
5.	Venezuela (1960-88)	33.83 (4.24)	-0.239 (-1.09)	0.579	1.89	554.34
6.	Philippines (1960-89)	9.87 (2.08)	0.665 (2.96)	0.816	1.53	140.58
7.	U.S.A. (1960-89)	6.58 (3.37)	0.64 (6.31)	0.643	1.45	12.7
8.	Japan (1960-89)	33.91 (12.65)	-0.024 (-0.455)	0.626	1.6	106.44

9.	Greece	5.81	1.155	0.848	2	68.65
	(1960-88)	(3.46)	(11.45)			
10.	Austria	0.191	0.99	0.849	1.74	22.36
	(1960-89)	(0.054)	(7.51)			
11.	Canada	3.66	0.899	0.716	1.94	27.44
	(1960-89)	(1.06)	(5.76)			
12.	Sweden	3.27	0.83	0.85	2.02	36.41
	(1960-88)	(0.86)	(4.87)			
13.	Germany	-0.05	0.86	0.885	1.49	28.46
	(1960-88)	(-0.01)	(5.15)			
14.	Netherlands	18.22	0.129	0.83	1.82	53.16
	(1960-89)	(3.563)	(0.833)			
15.	U.K.	9.13	0.535	0.46	1.66	4.77
	(1960-89)	(2.05)	(2.23)			
16.	France	2.03	0.9	0.89	2.33	18.81
	(1960-89)	(1.00)	(10.8)			
17.	Singapore	15.54	0.672	0.91	2.05	265.48
	(1960-89)	(1.915)	(2.99)			
18.	Sri Lanka	25.12	-0.247	0.76	1.89	207.55
	(1960-88)	(4.64)	-1.21			
19.	Thailand	27.73	-0.168	-0.0005	0.95	272.65
	(1960-88)	(4.89)	-0.649			
20.	Italy	-5.06	1.297	0.52	2.02	95.84
	(1960-89)	(-1.036)	(5.92)			

21. Zambia (1960-88)	27.68 (3.42)	-0.255 (1.085)	0.338	2.11	1164.88
22. Nigeria (1960-87)	14.5 (3.67)	0.122 (1.085)	0.68	1.68	282.15
23. Morocco (1960-88)	16.04 (2.80)	0.479 (2.50)	0.81	1.54	228.56
24. Ghana (1960-87)	8.11 (3.54)	0.165 (1.10)	0.69	1.93	156.24
25. Pakistan (1960-89)	17.56 (9.57)	-0.01 (-0.06)	0.47	1.74	44.76

Note: Figures in parentheses under the values of the coefficients are the respective t-values.
All regressions are done by Cochrane-Orcutt method to take care of serial correlation.

4. International Capital Market : Structure And The Mobility Of Capital The world is proceeding towards more integration regarding the movement of commodities and capital, though, for the latter, a number of restrictions remain. The number of countries which are truly open in capital account is very small. According to one study (Mathieson and Rojas-Suarez, 1993), of the 22 countries classified as industrially developed by the IMF in 1990, only nine allowed free capital movement, or these countries have capital account convertibility. Again, of the 178 members of the IMF, different types of restrictions on the trans-border movement of capital are seen in 140 countries. Even, members of the European Economic Union resort to the restrictions to the movement of capital wherever their currencies are threatened. Thus, the restrictions on the movement of capital across the political boundaries is an accepted paradigm in the international market and thus the Articles of Agreement of the International Monetary Fund declares:

Members may exercise such controls as are necessary to regulate international capital movements, but no member may exercise these controls in a manner which will restrict payments for current transactions or which will unduly delay transfer of funds in settlement of commitments, except as provided in Article VII, Section 3(b) and in Article XIV, Section 2 (Article VI, Section 3) [as quoted in Fieleke, 1994].

Though the tolerance to the imposition of restrictions on the movement of capital by a country in times of need is well accepted, it does not amount to inducement. Recently, Mexico ran into problem for adverse capital flight and short term movement of capital out of the country. For the stability of the currency (Peso) the country could impose restrictions on the outflow of capital. Though, as we will see later, this measure *per se* is not the solution to the problem as mentioned. The argument that controls should be imposed on the free movement of capital if the latter destabilises the economy requires precise identification of such capital flows. A capital movement is destabilising if that is motivated by an erroneous forecast of a foreign exchange rate. This happens due to the speculation on the likely movement of the exchange rate of the local currency in the near future. Faced with a situation like this, the authority can use any of the two alternative options. First, they can place restrictions on the movement of capital along with foreign exchange restrictions. Second, if destabilising flows are precisely identified, the authority can engage in offsetting capital movements to neutralise the effects of destabilising flows. Perhaps, economists favouring market solution rather than control on the movement of capital would argue in the following way:

"For example, suppose once again that the equilibrium exchange rate would remain constant but that private speculators have been selling the domestic currency in the mistaken belief that it should depreciate. In this case, the domestic monetary authorities could sell foreign currency in exchange for the now undervalued domestic currency, thereby limiting the depreciation of the domestic currency. To prevent their purchases of domestic currency from reducing their domestic money supply, the authorities could buy government securities from domestic residents in exchange for domestic currency. Once the domestic currency had returned to its equilibrium level, they could sell their previous purchases of it in exchange for foreign currency at a profit."

(Fieleke, 1994, p. 29)

But the type of money market subsumed in the above assertion may not exist in many developing countries. Physical restrictions on the movement of capital would be necessary then. The latter has often been supported from theoretical perspectives also. Some economists argue that control on the movement of capital can help the country achieve the following objectives: (a) the country can utilise domestic savings for the domestic capital formation (investment) and thus overall macroeconomic equilibrium can be established; (b) foreign direct investment in the domestic capital market can be controlled so that foreign influence in the domestic production structure is contained.

When capital is scarce due to low saving-income ratio, the authority wants to keep the limited surplus at home for productive investment. This has a welfare implications and the debate on the desirability of restrictions on the movement of capital ultimately boils down to this welfare implications. Almost all developing countries at different times have tried to contain the movement of capital in the domestic market. The results of these experiments are revealed in empirical results. One such good survey reveals the following (Mathieson and Rojas Suarez, 1993) :

— the collapse of the Bretton Woods System in the early 1970s created the expectations of large exchange rate adjustments and was accompanied by large-scale (often illegal) capital flows that overwhelmed even the most comprehensive capital control systems – when macroeconomic and financial conditions created substantial incentives for moving funds abroad, capital control in many developing countries were often of limited effectiveness in stemming capital flight during the 1970s and 1980s – recent studies suggest that the effectiveness of capital controls eroded more rapidly during the 1980s than during the 1960s and 1970s. (pp. 1-2)

(as quoted in Fieleke, 1994)

While literature gives plenty of examples about the failure of capital controls (Browne and McNelis, 1990; Otani, 1983), an opposite case is seen in Galy (1993) where it was shown that "capital controls were instrumental in reconciling the domestic and external objectives of monetary policy in Spain over the 1980s".

In today's world, thanks to the development of the information technology, monitoring of the different channels through which capital flows out of the country is extremely difficult. The situation becomes much more complex if the country is having a sizeable number of her citizens living abroad. In such a situation a mix of suitable monetary and fiscal policies is always better than the elaborate scheme of foreign exchange control if the objective of the authority is the containment of domestic capital at home.

The Country Cases Fieleke (1994) describes how countries like Spain and Portugal tried to stop the outflow of capital by placing restrictions. To restore stability in the exchange rate of the domestic currency peseta, the Bank of Spain introduced restrictions on the foreign exchange transactions of domestic banks in September, 1992. The regulations required the banks to deposit at the Bank of Spain for one year an amount equal to the domestic currency value of any new long position in foreign currencies with maturities at or before the spot value date. There was no interest on this deposit. Again, to discourage speculation by foreign banks, the regulation required that the commercial banks keep deposit with the central bank an amount equal to the value of new peseta-denominated loan to non-residents, excluding the loans related to commercial activities. Further, the domestic commercial banks were asked to maintain cash reserve equal to the full amount of new peseta liabilities in branches and subsidiaries of Spanish banks at home and abroad.

In the month of October, 1992, these restrictions were replaced by a new law which required the commercial banks to maintain a non-interest bearing deposits with the Bank of Spain for the peseta counter part of (i) same day or next day peseta sales to non-residents and also of (ii) new forward short positions in foreign currency contracted with foreign residents.

In the last week of November, 1992 the above restrictions also were abolished and Spanish peseta was devalued 6 per cent on November 23, 1992.

The experience of Portugal regarding the attempt by the central bank to maintain the stability of the exchange rate of its currency escudo with the help of putting restrictions on capital movement and foreign exchange dealings was same as in Spain. The escudo had to be devalued.

Is there any lesson in the experience of Spain or Portugal? Perhaps none, except the fact that the elaborate system of control as delineated above as a means of defending the foreign exchange value of domestic currency should not be made substitutes for the prudent monetary and fiscal policies required for the efficient functioning of the money and capital markets. Other developing countries also can learn from this.

Conclusion The analysis of the international mobility of capital has been followed in the context of a large number of countries including India. Though different aspects of the mobility question have come in the theoretical discussion in Section 2, the empirical part of this study examines the saving-investment correlation. The null hypothesis of perfect capital mobility (which amounts to zero correlation between saving and investment of a country) has been tested using the sophisticated tool of econometrics. The test has been conducted in the context of both time-series and cross-section data. The results broadly indicate lack of perfect capital mobility (except in a few cases) or financial integration, though complete auturky (where the correlation will be approximately unity) is also rare.

Indian Scene In the backdrop of the present study we can discuss Indian scene in some detail. The empirical results show that the estimated coefficient of (S/Y) ratio is 0.207 and this has level of significance as 7.8 per cent. Strictly speaking, the coefficient is not significantly different from zero at 5 per cent level of significance, which is a significant result in the case of an economy which, in any case, cannot be called open.

Even if we take this as a marginal case, the low value of the coefficient signifies an important level of financial integration of the domestic economy with the world. This aspect should be taken care in the formulation of the fiscal and monetary policies of the country.

Table 3:
Inflow of Foreign Capital

(U.S. Dollar billions)

Sources	1992-93	1993-94 (estimate)	1994-95
Remittances	2.7	3.8	6.0
FIIs	–	1.66	2.6
GDRs	0.086	1.46	2.3
FDI	`0.34	0.62	1.0
Offshore funds etc.	–	0.35	0.3

Source : Economic Times, March 14, 1995. p. 32
Note : FIIs = foreign financial institutions
FDI = foreign direct investment
GDRs = global depository receipts

The above observations point to another important phenomenon which we see in recent times, and that is, the nature of capital inflow into India. A close look at the table reveals that in recent times the quantum of remittances from the NRIs has increased tremendously. From $2.7 billion in 1992-93, it increased to $3.8 billion in 1993-94 and the projected figure of 1994-95 is $6.00 billion. Thus bulk of the capital inflow is coming from overseas Indians which is not of hot money type. Suspicion is quite high in some quarters that much of the remittances are the 'reverse capital flight' showing an increase in the confidence of NRIs in the Indian economy. Further, the huge inflow of remittances has other implications like the following :

First, the rigid exchange control regime along with stricter control on the capital movement prevailing in India in the last four decades had not been able to check the capital flight and Indians accumulated billions of U.S. dollars abroad through different channels. May be, a fraction of that is coming back in the present liberal atmosphere. This should be a lesson for the future conduct of the policies.

Second, the high level of remittances have negated to some extent the attempt of the government to reduce the inflationary impact of the capital inflow by lowering interest rates on NRI bank deposits, putting a cap on the Euro issues and restricting cash remittances from the GDRs. Perhaps, Reserve Bank of India will have to resort to open market operations in coming days to mop up excess liquidity. This is crucial for the stability of the exchange rate of rupee.

Third, the authority should initiate all the complementary measures of liberalisations so that the present climate is maintained. Further, suitable fiscal and monetary policies should be devised so that the capital flowing in are utilised in productive operations.

While we witness the inflow of capital, we should be mentally mature enough to see some amount of reverse flow in the future. After all, portfolio management is an individual operation.

Fourth, the attempt of rent-seeking on the part of foreign financial institutions in Indian capital market should be discouraged. This is possible only when we carry out necessary reforms in the price structure including the interest rates. Rather, we should encourage foreign direct investment in the domestic economy. This will serve two purposes simultaneously. Along with capital new improved technology will come into the Indian industrial sector. Also, an increasing presence of foreign firms will induce competition in the Indian industry which has a long term positive spill over effect.

Fifth, inflow of foreign capital, particularly of the short term nature, should be closely monitored and the monetary authority should be well aware about the foreign obligations. The full implications one can discern by analysing the impact of capital inflow into the countries of South Asia. While the topic has been explained in detail in Appendix B, we can simply say here that the central bank should remain fully informed about the short term obligations of the country.

Stability of Capital Flows and the Issue of Tax In the context of the South Asian currency melt down, some economists argue that short term capital inflows should be discouraged into a country as this is hot money in nature. Also there is a fresh debate whether a Tobin type tax should be imposed on capital flows both ways (Dooley, 1996; Garber, 1995). Clearly, two issues are involved: optimum level of capital inflow and desirability of the imposition of tax. Let us deal these two issues in turn.

One consensus is that the developing countries should get foreign capital to accelerate the growth rate of gross domestic product. Because of this all developing countries are eager to attract foreign capital. The question is whether the distinction is possible between short term and long term capital flows.The preference for long term capital comes because of the belief that long term flows, such as foreign direct investment, are guided by medium-term fundamentals of the economy and are less sensitive to the short term cyclical fluctuations in domestic or international interest rates.

The preference for short term capital flows is understandable, but it is difficult to design capital controls to target only short term capital flows. It is often not clear which capital flows are short term and which are long term. Standard classification in the international transactions like portfolio flows, direct investment etc, are not very informative regarding the volatility and liquidity of the flows. In fact the distinctiveness of these flows may be less than these categories suggest. Also in the face of controls in limiting short term capital inflows, if incentives are strong enough, even inflows that are perceived to be long term flows by policy makers may in fact be more liquid. For example if the foreign investors are interested to get out of the country, they can do that. As it is possible to create a 'synthetic sale' by obtaining a bank loan in the domestic currency that can be initiated quickly against the assets.

Prof. Tobin (1978) proposed a tax on the international flows of capital to make the capital flows more stable and less speculative. Also some control on external capital flows has become imperative for the maintenance of the independence in monetary policy with a fixed exchange rate regime. One proposal that has gained some popularity is the worldwide implementation of a tax on foreign exchange trading and on short term cross border bank loans. The argument is that such a tax would give countries more autonomy in monetary policy, raise the cost of speculative attacks on currency, and encourage investors to focus on longer term investment rather than short term speculation. The proposal is a modern vintage of Tobin's proposal (Garber and Taylor, 1995).

There are some practical problems with a Tobin tax. First, to make it effective, it would probably require to be imposed worldwide and at a uniform rate. Second, it has become easy to create a synthetic position through derivatives complicating effective tax on the foreign transactions. Third, imposition of tax on foreign currency trading will reduce liquidity considerably. These may not be good for the developing countries.

Empirical literature proves that capital control becomes ineffective in the long run as the agents try to dodge such measures when the pay-off is high. Also recent research suggest that countries that have capital controls in place often experience higher inflation and low real interest rate. This is another form of financial repression, and the authorities can more effectively tax captive domestic currency deposits through higher inflation (Grillietal, 1995).

Literature Cited Bayoumi, T, Saving - Investment correlations; immobile capital, government policy, or endogeneous behaviour? *IMF Staff Papers,* 37, 1990. 360-87.

Browne, F. X. and P. D. McNelis, Exchange Controls and Interest Rate Determination with traded and non-traded assets: the Irish-United Kingdom Experience, March 9, 1990. 41-59
Capiro, G. Jr. and D. H. Howard, Domestic Saving, Current Accounts, and International Capital Mobility, International Finance Discussion Paper 244, Federal Reserve System, Board or Governors, Washington, 1984 (as mentioned in Montiel, 1994)

Cuddington, John T. Capital Flight : Estimate, Issues, and Explanations, Princeton Studies in International Finance, Princeton University, Department of Economics, 1986. (mentioned in Montiel, 1994)

Dooley, Michael P. A Survey of Academic Literature on Controls over International Capital Transactions, *IMF Staff Papers,* 43 (4), 1996, 639-87.

Dooley, Michael, J. Frankel and D. Mathieson, International Capital Mobility : What do Saving-Investment Correlations tell us? *IMF Staff Papers,* 34, 1987, 503-30.

Edwards, S. and M. S. Khan, Interest Rate Determination in Developing Countries: A Conceptual Framework, *IMF Staff Papers,* 32, 1985 (September), 377-403

Feldstein, Martin, Domestic Saving and International Capital Movements in the Short Run and the Long Run, *European Economic Review,* 21 March-April, 1983, 129-51

Feldstein, M. and C. Horioka, Domestic Savings and International Capital Flows, *Economic Journal*, 90, June, 1980, 314-29

Feldstein, M. and P. Bacchetta, National Savings and International Investment, in B. D. Bernheim and J. B. Shoven (eds.), National Savings and Economic Performance, NBER Project Report, Chicago, Chicago University Press, 1991

Fieleke, Norman, S. International Capital Transactions : Should they be Restricted. *New England Economic Review*, Federal Reserve Bank of Boston, March April 1994, 27-39

Frankel, J. International Capital Mobility and Crowding out in the U.S. Economy : Imperfect Integration of Financial Markets or of Goods Markets? in R. W. Hafer (ed.), *How Open is the U.S. Economy*? Lexington, Mass, Lexington Books, 1986.

Frankel, J. Quantifying International Capital Mobility in the 1980s, in Bernheim and Shoven (eds.), National Saving and Economic Performance, Chicago, University of Chicago Press, 1991

Frankel, J. International Capital Mobility : A Review, *American Economic Review*, 82, May 1992, 197-202

Garber, P. and M. P. Taylor, Sand in the Wheels of Foreign Exchange Markets: A Sceptical Note, *Economic Journal*, 105, 1995, 173-180.

Golub, Stephen S. International Capital Mobility: Net Versus Gross Stocks and Flows, *Journal of International Money and Finance*, 9 December, 1990, 424-39

Grilli, V. and G. M. Milesi-Ferreti, Effects and Structural Determinants of Capital Controls, *IMF Staff Papers*, 1995, 42(3), 517-51.

Harberger, A. C., Vignettes on the World Capital Markets, *American Economic Review,* 70, Papers and Proceedings, 1980 331-7

Haque, Nadeem and P. J. Montiel, Capital Mobility in Developing Countries : Some Empirical Tests, *World Development,* 19(10), October 1991, 1391-98

Haque, N., K. Lahiri and P. J. Montiel, A rational expectations macroeconometric model for developing countries, *IMF Staff Papers,* September, 1990, 537-559

Galy, Michael, External Constraints on Monetary Management in M. Galy, G. Postor and T. Pujol, Spain : Converging with European Community, *Occasional Paper No. 101,* Washington, 1993, International Monetary Fund

Mathieson, D. J. and L Rojas-Suarez, Liberalisation of the Capital Account : Experiences and Issues, *Occasional Paper No. 103,* March, 1993, International Monetary Fund

Montiel, P. J., Capital Mobility in Developing Countries : Some Measurement Issues and Empirical Estimates, *The World Bank Economic Review,* September, 1994, 311-350

Murphy, Robert, Capital Mobility and the Relationshi p between Saving and Investment in OECD Countries, *Journal of International Money and Finance,* December 3, 1984, 327-43

Murphy, Robert, Productivity Shocks, non-traded goods and optimal capital accumulation, *European Economic Review,* 30, 1986, 1081-95

Obstfeld, M., Capital Mobility in the World Economy: Theory and Measurement, Carnegie-Rochester Conference Series on

Public Policy, 24, Special issue of *Journal of Monetary Economics,* 1986

Otani, Ichiro, Exchange Rate Instability and capital Controls : the Japanese Experience, 1978-81, in Bigman, David and T. Taya (eds.), *Exchange Rate and Trade Instability : Causes, Consequences and Remedies,* Cambridge, Mass Ballinger, 1983.

Penati, A. and M Dooley, Current Account Imbalances and Capital Formation in Industrial Countries, 1949-81, *IMF Staff Papers,* March 31, 1984, 1-24

Phylaktis, Kate, Capital Controls : The Case of Argentina, *Journal of International Money and Finance,* 7, September, 1988, 303-20

Sinn Stefan, Saving-Investment Correlations and Capital Mobility: On the Evidence from Annual Data, *The Economic Journal,* 102, September, 1992, 1162-70

Summers, L, Tax Policy and International Competitiveness, in J. Frenkel (ed.), International Aspects of Fiscal Policies, *NBER Project Report,* University of Chicago Press, 1988

Takagi, Shiuji, Rediscount Policy and Official Capital Flows: A Study of monetary control in Central America in the 1950s, *Canadian Journal of Economics and Political Science,* November 29, 1986, 475-85

Tobin, J. Domestic Saving and international capital movement in the long run and short run by M. Feldstein : Comment, *European Economic Review,* 21, 1983, 153-56

———, A Proposal for International Monetary Reform, *Eastern Economic Journal* , 1978, July-October, 53-59.

Westphal, U., Domestic Saving and international capital movement in the long run and short run by M Feldstein : Comment, *European Economic Review*, 21, 1983, 157-59

Wong, D. What do saving- investment relationshi p tell us about capital mobility, *Journal of International Money and Finance*, 1990, 60-74

Table 4 : Data of 25 Countries : Time-Series : 1960-89

MOROCCO	INDIA		PAKISTAN			GHANA		
YEAR	X	Y	X	Y	X	Y	X	Y
1960	0.172	0.869	0.137	0.907	0.226	0.826	0.106	0.884
1961	0.168	0.859	0.1-6	0.876	0.187	0.891	0.101	0.935
1962	0.178	0.856	0.16	0.88	0.158	0.87	0.118	0.917
1963	0.18	0.845	0.183	0.875	0.175	0.873	0.127	0.886
1964	0.177	0.848	0.195	0.885	0.181	0.845	0.108	0.873
1965	0.184	0.864	0.155	0.877	0.179	0.917	0.108	0.862
1966	0.192	0.877	0.174	0.875	0.129	0.922	0.107	0.883
1967	0.177	0.899	0.161	0.866	0.103	0.924	0.141	0.869
1968	0.166	0.88	0.161	0.87	0.111	0.872	0.176	0.825
1969	0.176	0.866	0.161	0.869	0.118	0.872	0.117	0.888
1970	0.182	0.835	0.158	0.869	0.141	0.865	0.159	0.873
1971	0.194	0.843	0.158	0.871	0.142	0.919	0.156	0.866
1972	0.178	0.833	0.156	0.873	0.071	0.874	0.126	0.875
1973	0.193	0.814	0.142	0.865	0.09	0.866	0.144	0.858

1974	0.208	0.834	0.129	0.904	0.13	0.91	0.206	0.788
1975	0.222	0.811	0.134	0.926	0.127	0.864	0.252	0.844
1976	0.221	0.777	0.185	0.892	0.089	0.915	0.281	0.899
1977	0.207	0.792	0.193	0.892	0.111	0.9	0.342	0.845
1978	0.221	0.752	0.179	0.912	0.054	0.96	0.257	0.866
1979	0.229	0.747	0.179	0.929	0.041	0.84	0.245	0.871
1980	0.228	0.826	0.185	0.922	0.055	0.912	0.242	0.871
1981	0.257	0.808	0.188	0.907	0.046	0.961	0.261	0.891
1982	0.235	0.802	0.193	0.917	0.034	0.963	0.282	0.867
1983	0.227	0.808	0.188	0.915	0.037	0.994	0.24	0.867
1984	0.231	0.806	0.183	0.923	0.069	0.934	0.253	0.878
1985	0.259	0.783	0.183	0.937	0.096	0.924	0.271	0.852
1986	0.243	0.796	0.188	0.891	0.097	0.936	0.245	0.851
1987	0.229	0.793	0.191	0.861	0.108	0.922	0.226	0.855
1988	0.244	0.774	0.182	0.873	—	—	0.236	0.832
1989	—	—	0.175	0.871	—	—	—	—

Note : X = Investment/Income ratio
Y = Consumption/Income ratio

Source : IMF

Table 4: Continued

	NIGERIA		ZAMBIA		ITALY		THAILAND	
YEAR	X	Y	X	Y	X	Y	X	Y
1960	0.108	0.949	0.237	0.582	0.247	0.77	0.307	0.828
1961	0.108	0.945	0.242	0.623	0.255	0.76	0.131	0.726
1962	0.121	0.927	0.227	0.682	0.254	0.766	0.185	0.836
1963	0.133	0.89	0.179	0.653	0.251	0.786	0.215	0.834
1964	0.16	0.88	0.115	0.611	0.227	0.786	0.201	0.818
1965	0.183	0.837	0.243	0.601	0.2	0.785	0.202	0.794
1966	0.167	0.845	0.289	0.569	0.196	0.792	0.236	0.749
1967	0.164	0.87	0.308	0.63	0.205	0.01	0.237	0.79
1968	0.152	0.881	0.324	0.677	0.203	0.797	0.252	0.802
1969	0.143	0.862	0.181	0.486	0.217	0.787	0.263	0.782
1970	0.157	0.84	0.296	0.568	0.293	0.779	0.256	0.813
1971	0.23	0.806	0.373	0.648	0.249	0.783	0.242	0.798
1972	0.294	0.787	0.353	0.631	0.243	0.753	0.217	0.801
1973	0.29	0.622	0.292	0.55	0.272	0.772	0.27	0.768
1974	0.264	0.652	0.364	0.541	0.301	0.758	0.266	0.774

1975	0.211	0.731	0.405	0.79	0.239	0.75	0.267	0.8
1976	0.218	0.685	0.238	0.711	0.269	0.772	0.24	0.796
1977	0.216	0.673	0.247	0.779	0.249	0.756	0.269	0.78
1978	0.18	0.826	0.239	0.795	0.241	0.753	0.282	0.757
1979	0.211	0.714	0.141	0.769	0.266	0.76	0.272	0.771
1980	0.218	0.739	0.233	0.807	0.27	0.772	0.264	0.79
1981	0.216	0.87	0.193	0.932	0.245	0.777	0.263	0.785
1982	0.18	0.895	0.168	0.821	0.235	0.791	0.231	0.794
1983	0.128	0.898	0.138	0.874	0.222	0.792	0.259	0.788
1984	0.62	0.91	0.147	0.815	0.23	0.788	0.249	0.787
1985	0.68	0.888	0.149	0.846	0.225	0.793	0.24	0.794
1986	0.92	0.909	0.238	0.762	0.207	0.79	0.22	0.784
1987	0.103	0.811	0.128	0.831	0.207	0.795	0.258	0.759
1988	—	—	0.107	0.87	0.215	0.794	0.275	0.721

1989	–	–	–	–	0.216	0.791	–	–

Table 4: Continued

	SRI LANKA		SINGAPORE		FRANCE		U.K.	
YEAR	X	Y	X	Y	X	Y	X	Y
1960	0.141	0.889	0.164	0.969	0.23	0.744	0.186	0.829
1961	0.137	0.873	0.116	0.994	0.229	0.747	0.183	0.822
1962	0.145	0.87	0.156	0.967	0.236	0.751	0.17	0.833
1963	0.157	0.86	0.175	0.933	0.236	0.759	0.173	0.832
1964	0.143	0.878	0.2	0.928	0.253	0.744	0.204	0.814
1965	0.125	0.871	0.219	0.896	0.249	0.741	0.198	0.812
1966	0.143	0.891	0.219	0.873	0.257	0.74	0.192	0.811
1967	0.152	0.876	0.222	0.864	0.256	0.74	0.197	0.814
1968	0.159	0.871	0.249	0.841	0.252	0.747	0.204	0.805
1969	0.193	0.87	0.286	0.797	0.261	0.746	0.199	0.797
1970	0.189	0.842	0.387	0.795	0.269	0.726	0.196	0.796
1971	0.171	0.849	0.402	0.79	0.262	0.727	0.19	0.797
1972	0.173	0.843	0.411	0.743	0.264	0.726	0.186	0.816
1973	0.137	0.875	0.392	0.731	0.272	0.719	0.219	0.806
1974	0.157	0.918	0.446	0.714	0.281	0.729	0.219	0.831

1975	0.156	0.919	0.376	0.714	0.234	0.752	0.184	0.834
1976	0.162	0.861	0.408	0.693	0.254	0.753	0.2	0.814
1977	0.144	0.819	0.362	0.685	0.244	0.746	0.197	0.798
1978	0.2	0.847	0.39	0.679	0.232	0.755	0.194	0.794
1979	0.258	962	0.434	0.647	0.237	0.757	0.197	0.8
1980	0.338	0.888	0.463	0.612	0.242	0.77	0.168	0.81
1981	0.278	0.883	0.463	0.583	0.219	0.791	0.151	0.822
1982	0.308	0.881	0.479	0.577	0.219	0.8	0.157	0.826
1983	0.289	0.962	0.479	0.55	0.199	0.803	0.165	0.827
1984	0.258	0.801	0.485	0.547	0.19	0.804	0.174	0.829
1985	0.238	0.881	0.425	0.594	0.189	0.805	0.172	0.819
1986	0.237	0.88	0.385	0.607	0.195	0.795	0.171	0.837
1987	0.233	0.872	0.39	0.6	0.2	0.798	0.179	0.834
1988	0.228	0.88	0.369	0.583	0.21	0.789	0.201	0.835
1989	—	—	0.359	0.573	0.213	0.783	0.203	0.835

Table 4: Continued

	NETHERLAND		GERMANY		SWEDEN		CANADA	
YEAR	X	Y	X	Y	X	Y	X	Y
1960	0.27	0.7	0.273	0.701	0.247	0.759	0.23	0.802
1961	0.27	0.714	0.272	0.706	0.242	0.753	0.212	0.08
1962	0.257	0.73	0.274	0.714	0.241	0.756	0.219	0.781
1963	0.245	0.75	0.263	0.723	0.242	0.756	0.228	0.786
1964	0.281	0.728	0.281	0.704	0.263	0.735	0.239	0.772
1965	0.267	0.729	0.286	0.714	0.269	0.74	0.265	0.076
1966	0.272	0.734	0.265	0.719	0.257	0.75	0.272	0.752
1967	0.269	0.731	0.23	0.735	0.248	0.752	0.243	0.769
1968	0.272	0.722	0.245	0.718	0.24	0.762	0.232	0.775
1969	0.281	0.775	0.261	0.709	0.243	0.761	0.024	0.773
1970	0.294	0.777	0.276	0.704	0.256	0.75	0.219	0.778
1971	0.278	0.775	0.267	0.713	0.23	0.758	0.229	0.778
1972	0.252	0.766	0.259	0.719	0.221	0.764	0.023	0.776
1973	0.243	0.718	0.252	0.717	0.224	0.759	0.245	0.755
1974	0.241	0.724	0.221	0.734	0.238	0.769	0.263	0.745
1975	0.206	0.76	0.198	0.773	0.242	0.759	0.256	0.774

1976	0.206	0.76	0.216	0.758	0.235	0.782	0.252	0.077
1977	0.216	0.77	0.21	0.766	0.204	0.812	0.244	0.783
1978	0.22	0.782	0.211	0.76	0.176	0.814	0.236	0.784
1979	0.216	0.792	0.234	0.758	0.2	0.81	0.254	0.765
1980	0.216	0.792	0.235	0.767	0.212	0.811	0.024	0.767
1981	0.183	0.784	0.21	0.781	0.183	0.824	0.254	0.769
1982	0.179	0.779	0.197	0.779	0.177	0.833	0.198	0.799
1983	0.184	0.777	0.204	0.774	0.172	0.811	0.199	0.802
1984	0.191	0.758	0.204	0.765	0.175	0.791	0.207	0.079
1985	0.198	0.753	0.195	0.761	0.189	0.794	0.208	0.799
1986	0.197	0.759	0.195	0.746	0.174	0.794	0.213	0.815
1987	0.196	0.775	0.196	0.748	0.184	0.797	0.218	0.805
1988	0.209	0.755	0.204	0.739	0.191	0.79	0.228	0.793
1989	0.211	0.743	0.216	0.722	—	—	0.235	0.08

Table 4: Continued

	AUSTRIA		GREECE		JAPAN		U.S.A.	
YEAR	X	Y	X	Y	X	Y	X	Y
1960	0.285	0.072	0.185	0.919	0.324	0.672	0.184	0.804
1961	0.284	0.709	0.2	0.881	0.378	0.638	0.177	0.809
1962	0.262	0.729	0.212	0.88	0.344	0.661	0.185	0.803
1963	0.259	0.739	0.214	0.854	0.348	0.67	0.188	0.798
1964	0.028	0.072	0.257	0.852	0.349	0.654	0.188	0.795
1965	0.028	0.725	0.263	0.845	0.32	0.668	0.02	0.786
1966	0.298	0.716	0.223	0.841	0.326	0.661	0.202	0.788
1967	0.276	0.732	0.224	0.854	0.355	0.645	0.019	0.802
1968	0.274	0.729	0.231	0.857	0.369	0.623	0.189	0.807
1969	0.271	0.717	0.259	0.819	0.377	0.61	0.191	0.804
1970	0.297	0.693	0.281	0.818	0.391	0.598	0.178	0.816
1971	0.297	0.696	0.279	0.805	0.358	0.616	0.187	0.809
1972	0.306	0.688	0.295	0.778	0.355	0.622	0.194	0.803
1973	0.309	0.688	0.358	0.749	0.381	0.619	0.201	0.786
1974	0.311	0.692	0.293	0.815	0.374	0.935	0.193	0.769
1975	0.026	0.734	0.27	0.827	0.328	0.673	0.168	0.813

1976	0.273	0.742	0.263	0.808	0.319	0.674	0.183	0.806
1977	0.279	0.748	0.264	0.818	0.309	0.675	0.199	0.8
1978	0.026	0.074	0.277	0.811	0.309	0.673	0.211	0.788
1979	0.266	0.738	0.302	0.797	0.325	0.683	0.205	0.787
1980	0.284	0.735	0.286	0.809	0.323	0.687	0.186	0.802
1981	0.263	0.075	0.254	0.854	0.313	0.681	0.193	0.796
1982	0.023	0.754	0.211	0.857	0.301	0.691	0.166	0.826
1983	0.022	0.767	0.219	0.855	0.283	0.698	0.166	0.835
1984	0.239	0.759	0.201	0.842	0.283	0.688	0.197	0.818
1985	0.234	0.764	0.215	0.859	0.284	0.678	0.185	0.835
1986	0.232	0.759	0.194	0.87	0.28	0.676	0.181	0.844
1987	0.024	0.755	0.175	0.889	0.29	0.672	0.179	0.848
1988	0.256	0.741	0.184	0.891	0.308	0.663	0.173	0.842
1989	0.259	0.736	—	—	0.323	0.656	0.169	0.84

Table 4 Continued

	PHILIPPINES		VENEZUELA		CHILE		MALAYSIA	
YEAR	X	Y	X	Y	X	Y	X	Y
1960	0.162	0.852	0.176	0.702	0.175	0.85	0.126	0.749
1961	0.181	0.859	0.172	0.68	0.18	0.9	0.143	0.801
1962	0.179	0.836	0.176	0.665	0.15	0.767	0.167	0.81
1963	0.196	0.831	0.17	0.658	0.188	0.85	0.162	0.822
1964	0.211	0.859	0.212	0.667	0.169	0.792	0.159	0.825
1965	0.209	0.858	0.208	0.695	0.174	0.789	0.157	0.799
1966	0.0198	0.855	0.2	0.705	0.173	0.804	0.157	0.804
1967	0.211	0.848	0.203	0.702	0.15	0.847	0.161	0.713
1968	0.214	0.84	0.273	0.654	0.154	0.854	0.158	0.81
1969	0.206	0.828	0.264	0.668	0.161	0.815	0.146	0.755
1970	0.215	0.792	0.296	0.659	0.222	0.889	0.203	0.78
1971	0.211	0.803	0.297	0.641	0.154	0.846	0.209	0.778
1972	0.208	0.814	0.312	0.655	0.43	0.913	0.213	0.798
1973	0.203	0.755	0.293	0.611	0.78	0.93	0.236	0.707
1974	0.251	0.762	0.24	0.513	0.212	0.782	0.293	0.713
1975	0.296	0.763	0.309	0.612	0.131	0.889	0.255	0.762

1976	0.313	0.747	0.344	0.642	0.128	0.829	0.228	0.677
1977	0.29	0.763	0.415	0.662	0.144	0.874	0.238	0.686
1978	0.29	0.762	0.428	0.703	0.178	0.855	0.267	0.678
1979	0.31	0.756	0.316	0.665	0.178	0.85	0.289	0.622
1980	0.307	0.753	0.247	0.671	0.21	0.832	0.304	0.671
1981	0.307	0.763	0.229	0.712	0.227	0.876	0.35	0.712
1982	0.288	0.786	0.259	0.772	0.113	0.906	0.373	0.714
1983	0.271	0.786	0.118	0.774	0.98	0.875	0.378	0.679
1984	0.174	0.832	0.175	0.713	0.136	0.874	0.336	0.645
1985	0.143	0.859	0.185	0.723	0.137	0.835	0.276	0.673
1986	0.132	0.852	0.209	0.801	0.146	0.816	0.26	0.679
1987	0.162	0.831	0.244	0.75	0.169	0.79	0.234	0.627
1988	0.174	0.822	0.273	0.797	0.17	0.758	0.261	0.636
1989	0.187	0.825	—	—	—	—	0.289	0.669

Table 4: Continued

	KOREA			KOREA	
YEAR	X	Y	YEAR	X	Y
1960	0.109	0.999	1975	0.271	0.819
1961	0.133	0.981	1976	0.253	0.768
1962	0.129	0.976	1977	0.286	0.73
1963	0.182	0.919	1978	0.331	0.712
1964	0.141	0.919	1979	0.36	0.718
1965	0.151	0.935	1980	0.317	0.762
1966	0.219	0.893	1981	0.295	0.761
1967	0.223	0.902	1982	0.286	0.75
1968	0.262	0.861	1983	0.288	0.714
1969	0.292	0.821	1984	0.298	0.695
1970	0.254	0.846	1985	0.293	0.693
1971	0.251	0.853	1986	0.283	0.66
1972	0.221	0.831	1987	0.295	0.634
1973	0.255	0.767	1988	0.306	0.617
1974	0.314	0.794	1989	0.345	0.634

IV

CAPITAL FLIGHT FROM INDIA DETERMINANTS AND ECONOMIC IMPLICATIONS

1. INTRODUCTION

Among The Inputs Of Production, capital is most mobile across the political boundaries. In an ideal situation when risk is absent in the case of investment in other countries and there is no restriction also on the mobility of capital, investors will put money in that country where return is the highest. This is how international capital market behaves and the premia on different categories of assets take care of the different kind of risks involved. This is portfolio management of a conscious investor. But in the literature we find one interesting situation which can be put in the following way : when the NRI based in the U.S.A. puts his/her money in an Indian bank, we call it international investment; but when an Indian puts his money in a foreign bank, we call it capital flight. As such there is little difference between the two situations. Whatever differences may remain can be discerned by studying the perceptions of the investors about the country they live in vis-a-vis the country they are sending their assets to. If we explore the motivations of the Indian citizen when he puts his money in the foreign bank, we may see any one or a combination of more than one of the following : (i) a perception that the present exchange rate of the domestic currency is over-valued and the depreciation is around the corner, (ii) the inflation rate is very high and the real rate of interest is negative, (iii) the budget deficit is high and potential future tax burden is high, (iv) the direct tax rate is very high and there is incentive to evade the taxes and (v) the security of the asset may be threatened in future.

A look at the list shows that return on the asset is not the main consideration. Further, political uncertainty and a potential threat of war can induce the movement of capital of the above type and this sort of "distress" movement of capital across political boundaries is known as capital flight and this is sharply distinguished from the normal overseas investment. Thus Indian corporate sector has been investing abroad for a long time and this overseas investment is not the subject of this study. But Indians are sending money abroad and keeping that in foreign banks since the 50s and even earlier through different channels which are not sanctioned by the laws. This is capital flight and the illegal nature of this also distinguishes it from the normal mobility of capital.

The history of capital flight is very old and fascinating. In 1997 Hong Kong was returned to China through a treaty in which the economic and politcal system of the island will be maintained for 50 years. If the perception about China becomes negative, and the rich become apprehensive about the motive of the ruling party in China, they can shift their capital abroad. Again, before the World War II, when Europe became suspicious about the Nazi rule in Germany, capital flight began from Germany to other countries. Prof. Kindleberger (1987; p. 22) has a fascinating story on this, which is like the following:

In 1937, on a train from Amsterdam to Paris-Emile Despres fell into conversation with a man who said his business had been getting capital out of Germany. There were, he said, three methods : one could buy a Reich bank official and get sterling in London; this was expensive but sure. Or one could bribe a bank clerk to get currency for deposits in large amounts, and get it out of Germany through the pouches of diplomatic officers of a number of small states. Or one could smuggle it out by train. The risk-return pay-offs by each method were related, and what was especially notable was that when there was a coup by the German authorities that temporarily blocked one method, the cost of using the others rose.

A close examination of the above story reveals that this may be repeated in any country at other times if situations warrant this. In the period of 1930s, two waves of capital flight took place across the Atlantic. In 1930-31, capital flight occurred from the U.S.A. to Europe and this was induced by the currency policies of the central banks of some countries in Europe. Towards 1937-38, reverse capital flight started from Europe to the U.S.A. and this was induced by the rise of Nazis in Germany and the shadows of war. Brown (1987) has explained the currency development in the major centres of the world and how that influenced the flight of capital.

Some economists relate capital flight with the flight of human capital or brain drain (Bhagawati 1964). Sometimes education in foreign universities of students from the developing countries like India becomes the cause of capital flight as the process of financing such education programmes suggests. One can see Indian students in the undergraduate programmes of American Universities. In the 70s and 80s normal remittance of dollars from India was not possible for undergraduate programmes. These students used to get dollars from their relatives in the U.S.A. or the "friends" of their parents. Now what is the mechanism that converted Indian rupees into steady flow of U.S. dollars is not mere speculations nowadays and it is one standard mechanism of capital flight. In the end if the student stays in the U.S.A. and resides there, then capital flight and brain drain get mixed up. And this sort of experience is not rare.

Capital flight is defined as the outflow of capital from a country to a destination considered to be safe by the decision making agents when the princi pal motivation is not to have higher return in a legal way but to keep the money beyond the long arm of the law of the country. Thus capital flight (CF) is the outcome of a deep maladies of the economic and political systems of the country. It came into the limelight of academic discussion in the early part of 1980s when it was seen that some Latin American countries were suffering simultaneously from huge amount of foreign debt and a large outflow of capital from the domestic economy. While the ethical part of the outflow of capital from the poor countries to the industrial economies needs no emphasis, the economics of the phenomenon requires explanations. This aspect will be explored in detail in this chapter.

The main objective is to explore the possible causes of the capital flight (CF), to explain the theoretical structure of the outflow of capital and to determine quantitatively the factors influencing the outflow. With this broad objective in mind the plan of this chapter is as follows: In Section 1 we will explain the capital flight in historical perspective along with the experiences of different countries. The different mechanism through which outflow of capital takes place will also be explained. Since the CF takes place without the sanction of law, any attempt to measure it depends to some extent on guesswork. Thus figures are never accurate and considering the gravity of the problem different researchers have come out with different measures of CF. These alternative measures will be discussed in Section 2. The theoretical frameworks giving the models of the estimation are put in Section 3, which also contains the empirical results. The last Section comes in the form of a conclusion.

2. Capital Flight : A Historical Perspective The world has been witnessing a great influx of refugees in Asia, Africa and Europe in recent times. Thousands of people are forced to leave their homes through persecution and these people carry precious metals and currency with them. This is one form of capital flight and our history is replete with incidents like this. In late 40s and early 50s people in millions migrated from eastern part of Bengal and West Punjab due to the partition of the country. Capital also flowed in along with them. This is comparatively a recent history.

In the 18th century the French Revolution induced a massive flight of capital from France to England and during the period 1789-1791 the refugee money pouring into the Bank of England led to an increase in the note-issuing by the country banks (Ashton, 1959, p. 168). But when the terror ended following the fall of Robespierre in July, 1794 and the collapse of the assignees paper money issued by the revolutionary government of France, 1790-95, a return movement of specie to France took place. The movement of specie to Britain from France began in 1789 and it increased in volume over the years. As Hawtrey (1919) points out, the mint that normally received £ 6,50,000 a year acquired £3.75 millions in 1793 and 1794. The prices began to be quoted in gold in Paris. There was an enormous profit to be made on importing gold as the premium on the local currency in 1795 was 20 per cent higher than the premium on the foreign bills (Hawtrey, p. 247).

Whether it is 18th century France or 20th century Bengal or present day Afghanistan, flight of capital is associated with some form of a "distress", though it need not always be the case. In the highly artificial atmosphere of rigid capital and exchange control, when local currency is highly over-valued, large scale trans-hpment of foreign currency takes place across political boundaries to capitalise gains in the differences of official exchange rate and black market rates.

Sometimes capital flight is seen in the perspective of the management of portfolio of assets. The latter may or may not be accumulated in a legal way. Assets accumulated through activities like bribery, financial fraud, corruption, smuggling of arms etc. are generally meant for capital flight when shifting these in foreign lands reduces the risks of detection. Even legal assets may be shifted abroad for tax evasion. In any case the magnitude of the capital flight depends on the nature and size of the underground economy of the country.

In the context of portfolio management Walter (1987) defines flight capital in the following way:

Correctly defined, capital flight therefore appears to consists of a subset of international asset redeployments or portfolio adjustments – undertaken in response to a significant perceived deterioration in risk – return profiles associated with assets located in a particular country – that occurs in the presence of conflict between the objectives of asset holders and governments. (p.105).

In the context of the above definition the motivations behind the flight of capital to foreign lands schematically come under the following categories : information and transaction costs, risks, confidentiality and expected returns.

In standard portfolio theory there is always a trade off between the risk and the return. The investor calculates the trade-off before getting into the option or selecting the type of the portfolio. This general consideration is complicated in the case of capital flight by an additional dimension of confidentiality regarding the location, size and the composition of the assets. When the accumulation of wealth does not have the legal sanction, confidentiality becomes important and the asset holder buys it at the cost of even negative return on the investment made. In general confidentiality is not a free good, and it is obtained at a price by putting the assets in a portfolio that yields the desired level of non-disclosure. The price is related to the secrecy and its magnitude is the low amount of return on the "secret" investment or even a negative return on the assets. One European banker estimates that much of the 4600 billion dollar deposited by foreigners in Swiss banks receives negative interest returns, implying that depositors were willing to pay a premium for security (Lessard and Williamson, 1987, p. 83).

The above gives the theoretical explanation of the rationale of keeping money abroad even when return is low and risk is high. Even a formal model has been in the literature to put the issue in a schematic form (Walter, 1987). According to Walter, when we keep the ethical issues apart, the acquisition of assets and holding of the same secretly by the individual engaged in capital flight can be thought of as a rational process on the part of the decision maker. This decision making process balances a number of perceived cost against benefits and the expected changes in these parameters are likely to change the behaviour of the investor. When we assume that the investors are risk-averse, other things remaining the same, they will generally choose portfolios incorporating greater confidentiality together with lower covariances in expected future total returns. Together with returns, confidentiality also becomes an attribute influencing the decision making process.

The above discussion helps to understand how the investor motivated to capital flight uses the conduits to send money abroad.

The Mechanism Of Capital Flight The mechanism of capital flight has three principal aspects : the transfer of asset from the country, the deployment of the asset, and the possible migration of the investor to the same destination. The modus operandi of the transfer of capital differs depending on the space and time. Also the cost of the operation is an important element in the determination of the mode of operation. The principal vehicles used for the transfer of capital and usual practices seen in different countries can be put into several broad categories, which are described below :

Capital Flight By Cash Movement According to a story narrated by Prof. Kindleberger (1987), he met a man in Switzerland in 1940 who had arranged five $100 bills from New York each week, which he sold for about $650. He then sent

$500 back by draft each week and lived on the difference. This is one method and during this period a large amount of capital flight from Europe to the U.S.A. took place through currency movements reported by banks, and also through covert mail exports of U.S. currency, and also through purchases of currency through intermediaries in New York that were hidden in safe deposit boxes. This is European capital flight, which is reflected in an increase in European holdings of U.S. currency.

Buying foreign currency at home is one form of capital flight. Similarly another form is selling domestic currency abroad. As noted by Kindleberger (1987), various German, Italian and Russian foreign exchange controls were evaded by selling the currencies abroad. The currencies transferred to foreign lands enter into the country again to buy commodities outside the purview of the law. Thus illegal currency movements involve smuggling, which are, most of the time, border trade to avoid high custom duties.

In the presence of strict exchange control, imports and exports of domestic currency are usually prohibited. Incoming non-residents furnish information regarding the possession of foreign currencies or other monetary instruments. Same information is collected from the outgoing ones and the differences are documented and these are to be explained by the persons with detailed documents. When the premium in the black market is high, incoming non-residents have an incentive to under report foreign currencies on arrival and over report on departure, though, in general, travellers are subject to physical search, seizure and criminal sanctions (Bhandari and Decaluwe, 1986).

One indication of the existence and operation of the underground economy in any country is disproportionately high amount of currency in circulation. Of course, the latter may also be due to lack of sufficient monetisation of the economy and the non-development of the monetary instruments. Thus in a country like India, if the currency in circulation is disproportionately high, it is difficult to conclude about the cause. But the present author came to know that for quite some time in 1997 a Rs. 500 bill used to bring Rs. 525 in the open market at Mumbai and the premium is due to the fact that for the transfer of huge amount of currency across the border a Rs. 500 bill is very convenient. In the international level, the U.S. dollar is the predominant vehicle currency. Federal Reserve data and the size of reported inter-bank international currency transaction indicate that a significant proportion of U.S. currency in circulation is actually held outside the United States (Hector, 1985).

The German mark and Japanese yen are nowadays supplementing the role of U.S. dollar. The existence of an underground economy and the flight of capital are interrelated and the high denomination currency is an instrument in this regard. The amount of currency in circulation is used for the measurement of parallel economy in a country (Gutmann, 1977). This is done by taking the difference between the actual amount of currency in circulation and the desired level of currency, when the latter is an estimate based on the income elasticity of the demand for cash balance of the concerned country.Two things are important here the degree of monetisation of the economy and the stability of the demand function of cash balance.

Capital Flight By False Invoicing When exchange rate is fixed and rigidly regulated, authorities also exercise exchange control and in such a situation the premium in the black market becomes high. Thus an exporter sees that for every U.S. dollar of export he is getting less in terms of local currency (determined by the over-valued official exchange rate) than what he would get in the unofficial free market. This is precisely the incentive of under-invoicing of exports and over-invoicing of imports (Bhagawati, 1964 and Gulati, 1987).

In the case of an export, the domestic exporter issues an invoice for an amount in foreign currency less than the agreed price. The foreign importer of the commodity places the difference in an account maintained by the exporter in a foreign based bank and officially remits the invoice amount, which is surrendered to the central bank to convert into local currency at the official rate. Thus the export figure of the exporting country and the import figure of the importing country will be sharply different over and above the f.o.b./c.i.f. factor. This difference is the capital flight, according to Bhagawati (1964). Similarly, in the case of imports, the amount of invoice supplied by the foreign supplier is much higher than the price agreed upon with the importer. The importer gets the necessary license of the foreign currency equivalent to the invoice amount and remits the same to the foreign supplier, who takes the agreed price and places the balance in an account of the foreign bank.

In both the cases of false invoicing, the trader becomes successful to shift money abroad and capital flight takes place. From the perspective of the country, both the prices of exports and imports are shadow prices and the terms of trade changes which is equivalent to the depreciation of the currency. Thanks to invoicing for the export evaluated in domestic currency less amount of dollar accrues to the central bank, while for imports, more foreign currency goes out-both cases are equivalent to devaluation and also a deterioration of the terms of trade.

Walter (1987) points out that capital flight through false invoicing can be multi plied by a method called "round tri pping". Traders accumulate assets abroad by false invoicing. Some of these assets are brought inside the country by suitable monetary instruments. This money is then converted into domestic currency in the black market to realise the premium. The gains in local currency can then be utilised for false-invoiced transactions in future. The incentive to do this comes from two sources – over-valued exchange rate and a rigid tax-subsidy system.

Capital Flight By The Transfer Of Precious Metals

When the economy is subjected to a high rate of inflation people lose faith in the credibility of the currency. They convert this into gold and some other valuable objects. Again, money accumulated through illegal means are often stashed away in foreign land in the form of gold and other valuable things. The economy suffers and the surplus of the country is invested elsewhere. The story of Philippines and some Latin American countries point to similar phenomenon. The capital flight from Philippines involved the Marcos family and other capitalists. Press report in July, 1988 indicated that Marcos had offered to repatriate $ 5 billion to the Philippines if the family was allowed to return to the country without any legal prosecution (Boyce, 1992). In fact, the World Development Report, 1985 published by World Bank describes in detail how the ruling families in some countries have siphoned off wealth from the country and kept abroad in case they are to flee the country. The recent currency meltdown in some South Asian countries like Thailand, South Korea etc. has also been associated with a substantial capital flight from these countries. This is an organised plunder of the economy.

The above paragraphs describe several forms of capital flight. Most of these phenomena happen in the context of a rigid exchange control regime with zero mobility of capital. When capital mobility is allowed, capital flight can occur through the normal channels of international payments, i.e., through bank transfer from a local branch of a foreign bank to a foreign affiliate. Even when exchange control exists, such bank transfer can cause capital flight may be at a price. But money generated through criminal activities cannot be transferred through banks for fear of detection.

The Economics Of Confidentiality We have mentioned earlier that in some businesses confidentiality or secrecy is a scarce item and it has a price. The supply of secrecy comes from institutions with active help from the legal system of the countries. The latter generally supply secrecy in two ways. First is the domestic bank secrecy laws, which prohibit insight by both the national and foreign authorities. The second is the blocking statutes and these prevent the disclosure, copying, inspection or removal of the documents located in the host country in compliance with orders or requests of foreign countries. Apart from the traditional tax havens a number of countries like the U.K., South Africa, West Germany, Austrália and Norway have comprehensive blocking statutes to guard their sovereignty from the extraterritorial reach of foreign countries.

***Table 4.1:* List of countries or centres regarded as tax havens**

Caribbean and South Atlantic	Europe, Middle East and Africa
Antigua	Austria
Bahamas	Bahrain
Barbados	Channel Islands
Belize	Gibraltar
Bermuda	Isle of Man
British Virgin Islands	Liberia
Cayman Islands	Leichteustein
Costa Rica	Luxembourg
Flakland Islands	Monaco
Grenada	Netherlands
Montserrat	Switzerland
Auguilla	Asia-Pacific
Netherland Autilles	Cook Islands
Nevis	Guam
Panama	Hong Kong
St Kitts	Maldives
St Lucia	Nauru
St Vincent	Vanuatu
Turks and Caicos Islands	Singapore
Uruguay	Tonga

Source : Walter (1985; p. 92)

We see that some countries are the "passive" suppliers of

secrecy at the international level and their legal system facilitates the process. Apart from that, recently a number of countries have become active suppliers of secrecy services. The reasons for this development are largely economic in nature.

First, thanks to socio-economic and political reasons, ethnic strife or civil war has been going on in a number of countries. This has created a large market for arms. Along with arms, narcotics trade is also flourishing. This trade requires financing and the demand of this type of secrecy is high in volume. Since established banks with reputation do not accept this type of business, some small countries have set up centres to supply this type of secrecy.

The reason why the small countries have assumed this role is that the revenue generated this way is utilised to promote economic development. Most of these countries are so small that apart from tourism they cannot have an adequate infrastructure for meaningful industrial development. Further, these economies are geographically isolated and dependent on the export of a limited number of goods. This isolation and vulnerability to climatic conditions induce these countries to open their economic system to tourism and financial secrecy business. On pure economic terms, such businesses have positive contribution to the economic growth of these regions. In the name of professionalism, the ethics of business are often violated and laundering of money generated through dubious means is a standard allegations against such centres. One important U.S. study (reported in Walter, 1985) observes this:

Africa, Central America and the Caribbean Islands are the areas most vulnerable to the involvement in politically corrupt or direct criminal matters where the headquarters of big U.S. banks have little control. Among the three regions mentioned, the Caribbean is the worst so far as shady deals are concerned. That appraisal conforms to the impression of gross inadequacies, improper influence, and reported criminal involvement in the

Caribbean involving some banks, local officials, assorted traveling highway men, narcotics traffickers and the like (Permanent Subcommittee on Investigations, Committee on Government Affairs, United States Senate, Crime and Secrecy : The Use of Offshore Banks and Companies, Washington, D.C., 1983). Inspite of this revealation little has been done so far to cleanse this area of international financial system because of the complex domestic legal system of the havens and sovereignty issues.

Nowadays safe havens are many and the laundering of dirty money is not costly enough to reduce its demand. The process is facilitated by at least two developments in the international banking field the innovation of new monetary instruments and the rapid advance of information technology. Within a very short time millions of U.S. dollars can be shifted from one place to other through coded messages and at a very low cost. While detection of this type of movement of cash is difficult, the investment opportunities of this money in the underground business of the world is not really limited. This reminds one of the maxim that money has no colour.

The Causes Of Capital Flight The first truth of capital flight is that it is injurious to the country from which capital flees. The second truth of it is that it is not the cause but the consequence of a set of factors created in a country over time. Many developing countries are seen to follow a set of fiscal and monetary policies which are not consistent. Leaving aside the country-specific variations, the common features can be put together to have a stylized picture. Generally the government sector suffers from fiscal imbalance and the fiscal deficit is covered by monetisation. The continuity of this creates two forces : one is the inflation and other is the fear of potential high taxation in future. Economic agents now take decision to guard against these twin evils. As inflation erodes the purchasing power of the currency, a very high inflation leads to a flight from domestic currency. Further, the economic agents keep their savings in such a way that these become immune from future taxation. The first option serves this purpose also and buying foreign currency is one form of capital flight.

Further, to supply cheap capital to the corporate sector and to the government sector, the nominal interest rate is kept at a low level, and thus real rate of interest becomes very low and often negative. So financial investment at home fetches very low or negative return. This induces investment abroad to avoid financial repression at home.

Another feature of such countries is the fixed exchange rate regime and a rigid exchange control with zero mobility of capital. The domestic currency often remains over-valued and there is the expectation of the depreciation of the domestic currency since the premium in the black market remain very high. This type of economic situation induces currency conversion to foreign currency, which is capital flight again.

The above description of stylized facts suggest a link between the budget deficit, monetary imbalance and external disequilibria and these are the ideal conditions for capital flight (Dornbusch, 1985; Pinto, 1989).

Apart from the economic explanation given above there are some historical experiences in some countries where capital flight has taken place in some unique fashion. Boyce (1992) has examined a hypothetical linkage between capital flight and external debt disbursement in the case of Philippines during 1962-86. Econometric analysis indicates some type of linkages and it suggests that large sums of capital flowed into and out of the country through a "financial revolving door". While huge inflow of capital took place for investment in industry or the infrastructure construction, a significant amount of that had been siphoned away and kept in foreign land by the all powerful oligarchy that ruled the country. The Philippines' model of capital flight as examined by Boyce explores the causality between capital flight and external debt from both angles and some statistical link has been established. A larger amount of debt disbursement has led to a greater capital flight, and more capital flight has led to a larger debt disbursement. One current example is China as some economists believe, that the large inflow of foreign capital through foreign direct investment (FDI) is also associated with a very high figure of "net errors and omissions" towards the closing of the balance of payments. A closer look in the country pages of International Financial Statistics (IMF) will reveal this. This is a sign of capital flight. Capital flight is to some extent related to the instability of the political system. It is seen that when macro-economic policies either for stabilisation of the economy or for structural reforms are not politically supportable, the rich get panicky about the safety of their financial fortune, and in the quest for safety they keep their money abroad. Thus both political and financial stability are necessary to keep the capital at home.

2. Different Measures Or Capital Flight Much of the flight of capital happens silently and beyond the documentation procedure of the national income statistics. But considering the severity of the issue and the magnitude of the problem some attempts have been made in the literature to measure the quantum of capital fleeing the country. The major attempts are World Bank's method (World Bank, 1985), Cuddington (1986), Dooley (1988), Morgan Guaranty (1986), Khan and U.L. Haque (1987), Erbe (1985), and Cline (1986). These alternative measures of capital flight (CF) try to capture that amount of capital fleeing the country which is different from "normal" capital flow (both ways) in private sector transactions. One way to make this distinction is to examine the extent to which private sector capital flows are two-way flows or one-way flow. If it is found that private sector capital account credits are much higher than the private sector capital accounts debits, then this is not the "normal" two-way flow of funds and capital is fleeing the country. While this distinction is useful conceptually, data problems limit its usefulness when one tries to implement this. Considering that some areas of CF remain grey, any measure of CF gives only an approximation to the size of the flow. This is an important *point in the CF literature.*

World Bank (1985) employs the broadest definition of capital flight and it takes the inflows of capital in the form of an increase in the external debt and net foreign direct investment and it subtracts from these inflows the current account deficit and the increase in the official reserves. It then takes the difference between these inflows and the extent to which they are used to finance the deficit in the current account and an increase in reserves as the reflections of an increase in net foreign claims by the private sector. According to World Bank this increase in net foreign asset is the measure of capital flight. Following this definition World Bank has measured the flight of capital in several countries (Table 4.2).

Professor Dooley (1986) has proposed that the stock of claims held on non-residents that do not generate investment income reported in the balance of payments be taken as a measure of capital flight. The implicit assumption is that the interest earned on legal and normal capital outflow will be reflected in the balance of payments. Once money is stashed away in illegal way, it earns interest and this interest also remains in foreign land and it is not reported in the balance of payments. Thus one can approximate capital flight by capitalising the stream of reported investment income and subtracting this from total external claims. This definition depends on the global management of investor's portfolio which are not reported to the government. If the outflow of capital takes place legally, then there is no capital flight.

***Table 4.2:* Capital Flight and Gross Capital Inflows in Selected Countries, 1979-82**

(Unit. billion of U.S. dollars)

Country	Capital Flight (1)	Gross Capital inflow (2)	2 as % of 3 (3)
Venezuela	22.0	16.1	136.6
Argentina	19.2	29.5	65.1
Mexico	26.5	55.4	47.8
Portugal	1.8	8.6	20.9
Turkey	0.4	7.9	5.1
Korea	0.9	18.7	4.8

Source : World Bank (1985), p. 64
Note : Gross Capital inflows are defined as the sum of changes in gross foreign debt (public and private) and net foreign direct investment.

But Cumby and Levich (1987) point out that the definition of Dooley suggests that the loss of national utility from the flight of capital comes not from the diversion of domestic capital to offshore investment, but from the foreign exchange receipts upon repatriation of offshore earnings.

Morgan Guaranty (1986) defines capital flight as a residual, and in addition to the current account deficit and the increase in official reserves, it subtracts the increase in short term foreign assets of the banking system from total inflow of capital. Thus when banks accummulate foreign assets, it is not the flight of capital by Morgan definition, but when other agents do the same, it becomes the capital flight.

While evaluating Morgan definition Cline (1986) argues that income from tourism and border transaction should be excluded from current account earnings and these earnings are beyond the controlling power of the relevant authority. Further, he argues that income accruing to the capital invested abroad should not be included in capital flight and for the same reasons as in the case of tourism income.

Cuddington (1986) uses a different approach for the measurement of capital flight and he concentrates on short term capital flows, as he is interested to examine "hot money" funds that responds quickly to changes in economic situations. He defines capital flight as the acquisition of short term external assets by non-bank private sector and it is measured by adding selected short term capital items to the errors and omissions.

Like Dooley (1986) Khan and U.L. Haque (1987) has tried to distinguish capital flight from normal capital flows that follow portfolio diversification at the global level by the domestic residents. In normal situation there are two-way capital flows among countries and taking one way flow as capital flight will be an inaccurate measure. To overcome this problem both Dooley (1986) and Khan and U. L. Haque (1987) have attempted to identify foreign assets as flight capital that generate income which are not reported. This type of fund once out of the country is lost for ever.

Another measure is of Erbe (1985) which is broad in nature just like the World Bank. Bhagawati (1964) uses a definition of capital flight which is based on the illegal capital exports by mis-invoicing of imports and exports. This can be measured by comparing the partner country data. Further Bhagawati, Krueger and Wibulswasdi (1974), on the basis of 1966 trade statistics, has come to the conclusion that under-invoicing of exports seemed to be used as a mechanism of capital flight while over-invoicing of imports was less frequently used. Gulati (1987) has followed this mechanism to measure flight capital for several countries. The incompatibility of the partner country trade statistics was first raised by Morgenstern (1950) while discussing the importance of accuracy of economic observations.

Dooley, Helkie, Tryon and Underwood (D-H-T-U) (1983) develops a methodology for the measure of capital flight and it consists of comparing the "financing needs" of a country with the "financial inflows" available to her in a given period. The difference is termed as capital flight. Here financing needs of a country consists of current account imbalances and changes in the international resources including the assets of the commercial banks. Again, financial inflows consist of increases in external debt along with foreign direct investment. The D-H-T-U methodology has been used by other researchers for the measurement of flight capital (Dornbusch, 1985; Diaz-Alejandro, 1984).

The different measures of capital flight remind one of the proverbial story of seven blind men trying to understand the physical properties of an elephant by its different limbs. Without being swayed by the outcome of the story we can take the moral of it that any scientific approach tries to approximate reality.

Following Cumby and Levich (1987) we can compare the different measures of capital flight with the help of the following table which are items taken from standard tables of International Finance Statistics (IMF):

Table 4.3

India : Some External Economic Indicators

(Unit : U. S. dollar million)

		1980	1989
A.	Current Account Surplus	-1785	-6826
	1. Excluded items	–	–
B.	Net foreign direct investment	–	–
C.	Private short term capital	-181	2421
D.	Portfolio Investment : bonds and equities	–	–
E.	Bankg system Foreign Asset (minus signifies an increase)	6872.64	2265.93
F.	Change in reserves (minus signifies an increase)	-488	-1040
G.	Errors and Omissions	-361	-285
H.	Change in Debt	972.3	-659.34

Table 4.4

Capital Flight: Different Measures :

Country : India

(U. S. dollar million)

		1980	1989
1	World Bank : H+B+A+F	-1300.7	-8525.34
2	Morgan : H+B+A+E+F	5571.94	-6259.41
3	Cline : Morgan-excluded i in A	–	–
4	Cuddington : (-G-C)	542	-2136

Note : H means change in debt as in Table 4.3 and so on.

While different methods compute the extent of capital flight of a country differently, we get sharply different estimates for the same country. In the present study we have adopted World Bank and Cuddington estimates for the measurement of capital flight from India.

In today's world of globalised capital market which is equipped with modern machines of information technology, residents of different countries can arbitrage an actual or an expected tax differential at little cost. When they do so, this induces an adjustment of individuals' financial positions across political boundaries and through this process, huge amount of capital flight may take place either legally or illegally. In the extreme situation when the residents of a country have less faith on their government regarding future taxation on their assets compared to the non-residents, offshore financial centres will be used extensively for financial intermediation and in this situation capital flight will be a universal problem. An efficient and pragmative tax system with selective incentives on savings can reduce the risks of capital flight in today's world.

The reported underground economy of different countries partly induces the flight of capital across the political boundaries. As the size of the informal sector is relatively large in the developing countries, who also suffer from the scarcity of investible resources, the large size of the underground economy with huge potential of capital flight in one pretext or another make the case of economic growth a difficult proposition. Some countries in Latin America and South Asia (e.g. Mexico, Argentina, Philippines, etc.) are examples in this regard. Only very recently, the governments of these countries have become conscious about the need for thorough economic reforms to check the outflow of capital.

Measurement Of Capital Flight From India Following the definitions explained in Tables 4.3 and 4.4, the measurement of capital flight from India is done which is based on the information in Table 4.5. Thus the calculation is done with the help of three measures the World Bank, Cuddington and Morgan.

There are several features of the measures of capital flight from India. While the Cuddington measure is very much conservative, the Morgan measure is much more inclusive than the World Bank one. Thus the quantity of capital flight from India is much higher according to Morgan measure compared to World Bank.

Second, as suggested before, the nature of the problem of flight capital is such that precise estimate is impossible and the quantities indicated in different measures give some idea about the problem. These at best approximate the truth that these can be utilised for any scientific study in the absence of any better alternative.

Third, there are very high fluctuations in the quantum of flight capital over the years and there is absolutely no systematic pattern. As we will see, this is not unique for India and other countries also experience this type of fluctuations. In some years both the inflow and the outflow of capital may happen simultaneously as a large group of agents are involved in this game of international transactions. Various economic events, both domestic and international in nature, influence the mobility of capital and the dimension of the flow. Thus when the price of gold and silver fluctuates in the European markets, or there has been a significant change in the custom duty and/or in other taxes, there may be a diverse movement of capital across the political boundary depending on the interests of the agents and the changes in the relative prices. So it is quite possible that when one agent is inducing the inflow as capital without the latter being reported, other agents may transfer money abroad being influenced by another set of economic variables.

Capital Flight Through Mis-invoicing Of Trade Two things bother the traders in the field of international transactions: one is the fixed and overvalued exchange rate of the currency, and the second is the higher rate of tariff on imports. Regarding the first, many a currency enjoy dual exchange rate system, the second being the unofficial one. When the premium in the unofficial market is high, the exporter becomes induced to encash a portion of the export earnings in the unofficial market. This is done by under-invoicing the export and the country receives the reduced value of the export earnings in foreign currency. The balance is either kept in foreign banks abroad or brought back into the country through illegal means. In either care the central bank is denied the foreign exchange.

Again, if the tariff rate is too high, the importer can avoid a portion of the tariff by under-invoicing the imports. Otherwise, over-invoicing is a standard weapon to transfer capital abroad.

For the present study, the extent of mis-invoicing of trade in the case of India has been studied by comparing data of partner-country basis in the case of India's trade partners like the U.K., the U.S.A., Germany, Japan, the former U.S.S.R., Hong Kong and Singapore. Taken together, these countries account for an overwhelming percentage of total international trade of the country. The source of the partner country data is the International Trade Statistics and the unit is the U. S. dollar million in all cases.

One standard source of discrepancies between partner country data is the c.i.f./f.o.b. conversion. This may account for 10 per cent of the value, but the percentage is not uniform. Regarding the arbitrary nature of the conversion factor, this has not been attempted here, but only the difference (showing approximately the size of misinvoicing) has been shown. This is done because the measurement of capital flight has been done through other methods.

Thus the difference between the value of exports of India to the U.S. and the value of imports of that country from India is explained by the transport cost which is the c.i.f. /f.o.b. factor. It can be 10 per cent or something else depending on the distance and the nature of the cargo. Whatever may be the exact figure of the c.i.f./f.o.b. factor, very large gap between the partner country trade data cannot be explained by this. Two practices are cited in this regard.

First, in many developing countries one widely prevalent practice is the under-invoicing of exports as explained above. In this the exporter reports to the central bank a lower value of the export than what is agreed upon and the importer on the other side keeps the balance in a separate account to be utilised by the exporter later on. In all the tables showing the partner country data large amount of under-invoicing of exports are seen in Indian trade with the U.S.A., the U.K. and Germany in particular. In the case of former U.S.S.R., the amount of mis-invoicing is minimum on non-existent. The reason is perhaps state level trading on the side of U.S.S.R. though in the case of some years some unnatural figures are derived.

In some cases over-invoicing of exports has happened in some years. In the year 1989 over invoicing of exports of India is very much common in India's trade with the U.S.A., Japan, the U.K. and West Germany. One explanation may be the existence of subsidy on exports. As there is a trade off between potential depreciation of the domestic currency yielding a high premium in the black amrket, and the realisation of subsidy which is *ad valorem* on the value of exports. In the tables on partner country data (Tables 4.7 - 4.13) column (4) shows the extent of under-invoicing of exports which is to be modified by the relevant c.i.f./f.o.b. factor.

Second, the common perception in the developing country is the over-invoicing of imports and this is done for the same reasons, i.e., transferring capital to the foreign country. Column (7) in Tables (4.7-4.13) shows the difference between the value of Indian imports and the value of exports of the partner country in the same year. Other things remaining the same. the figures in column 5, when reduced roughly by 10 per cent, should correspond to the respective figures in column 6. This is not the case in the tables. Rather we find that in a number of years for many countries there have been under-invoicing of imports in India. This is understandable. When the tariff on imports is too high, a lot of money can be saved by putting the value of imports on the lower side compared to the price agreed upon. The balance is paid to the foreign seller out of separate account kept overseas. Obviously, this type of balancing act required under-invoicing of exports to generate money abroad unreported to the government authority. A high tariff-high-subsidy system in the field of international trade not only distorts the domestic price structure of the country, but it induces the misinvoicing of exports and imports together leading to a situation of capital flight. The total quantum of misinvoicing for every country has been calculated and placed in column 8 of the tables (Tables 4.7 -4.13). The figures in column 8 give some idea about the quantum of capital flight according to Bhagawati (1964). Further, this exercise gives some expirical support to the measurement of flight capital by other methods like those of World Bank and others.

***Table 4.5:* Some Indicators of India's External Economy**

(Unit: U.S. dollar million)

Year	Current Account Surplus	Direct Foreign Investment	Non-Bank short term capital	Portfolio Investment	Banking System Foreign Asset	Total Reserve Minus Gold	Net errors and omissions	Foreign debt
1965	-1348	-	161	-	167.54	319	102	5468.06
1966	-930	-	236	-	66.25	365	24	6115.36
1967	-1121	-5	13	-	39.75	419	-103	6796.07
1968	-664	3	18	-	157.32	439	-191	7389.87
1969	-230	-10	-99	-	648.23	683	-36	8139.96
1970	-411	6	-	-	857.97	763	-4	8559.93
1971	-653	-1	70	-	1057.84	942	-80	9384.53
1972	-167	3	-45	-	1274.75	916	-239	8816.83
1973	-546	-13	-	-	1340.97	849	-34	7154.70
1974	1200	-6	17	-	981.60	1028	-275	7877.3
1975	-148	-10	11	-	1164.09	1089	-439	8503.97
1976	1571	-8	-106	-	2601.05	2792	-290	9694.85

1977	2108	-	-220	-	5177.24	4872	-129	0951.39
1978	683	-	122	-	6765.99	6426	432	455.79
1979	48	-	129	-	7967.62	7432	302	2596.43
1980	-1785	-	-181	-	6872.64	6944	-361	13568.73
1981	-2698	-	66	-	4462.03	4693	-325	12957.47
1982	-2524	-	-659	-	2293.96	4315	369	13639.19
1983	-1953	-	519	-	1477.17	4937	-850	13894.98
1984	-2343	-	275	-	2200.63	5842	368	12930.69
1985	-4179	-	-60	-	2309.72	6420	500	14918.63
1986	-4597	-	-504	-	2431.03	6396	197	15470.2
1987	-5192	-	1123	-	2453.99	6454	-409	18032.15
1988	-7148	-	2016	-	2374.74	4899	-112	17225.23
1989	-6826	-	2421	-	2265.93	3859	-285	16565.89
1990	-	-	178	-	4199.63	1521	-443	17622.97
1991	-	-	-	-	3417.97	3627	-	-

Note : Source : Direction of Trade Statistics, IMF.

***Table 4.6:* Capital Flight from India**
(Unit : U.S. dollar million)

Year	World Bank Measure	Cuddingyton Measure	Morgan Measure
1967	-391.29	90	-315.54
1968	-47.20	173	110.12
1969	754.09	135	1402.32
1970	84.97	4	942.94
1971	349.60	10	1407.44
1972	-757.70	284	517.05
1973	-2288.13	34	-947.16
1974	2095.60	258	3077.2
1975	529.67	428	1693.76
1976	4456.88	396	7057.93
1977	5444.54	349	10621.78
1978	2741.40	-554	9507.39
1979	2194.64	-431	10162.26
1980	-1300.70	542	5571.94
1981	-5560.26	259	-1098.23
1982	-2220.28	290	73.68
1983	-1075.21	331	401.96
1984	-2402.29	-643	-201.66
1985	-1613.06	-440	696.66
1986	-4069.43	307	-1638.4
1987	-2572.05	-814	-118.06
1988	-6399.92	-1904	-4025.15
1989	-8525.34	-2136	-6259.41

Table 4.7: Partner Country Data on Trade: India and the U.S.A.

(Unit: U.S. dollar million)

Year	Indian Exports	U.S.A. Imports (3-2)	Difference	Indian Imports	U.S.A. Exports	Difference (5-6)	Total Misinvoicing (4+7)
(1)	(2)	(3)	(4)	(5)	(6)	(7)	(8)
1975	477	621	144	1384	1290	94	238
1976	590	801	211	1324	1135	189	400
1977	689	865	176	846	779	67	243
1978	901	1080	179	928	948	-20	159
1979	899	1148	249	971	1167	-196	53
1980	1085	1210	125	1624	1689	-65	60
1981	1204	1325	121	1922	1748	174	295
1982	1384	1522	138	1756	1599	157	295
1983	2122	2334	212	2011	1828	183	395
1984	2488	2737	249	1727	1570	157	406
1985	2253	2479	226	1806	1642	164	390
1986	1778	2465	687	1430	1536	-106	581
1987	2114	2725	611	1503	1464	39	650

1988	2507	3153	646	1723	2490	-767	-121
1989	4424	3551	-873	2813	2463	350	-523
1990	2694	3421	727	2635	2486	149	876
1991	2922	3429	507	1891	2003	-112	395
1992	3696	4066	370	2106	1914	192	562

Note: Column (4) is under-invoicing of exports and thus (4) = (3) - (2)

Column (7) is over-invoicing of export less and thus (7) = (5) - (6)

Table 4.8: Partner Country Data: India and the U.K.

(Unit: U.S. dollar milllion)

Year	Indian Exports	U.K.'s Imports	Difference	Indian Imports	U.K.'s Exports	Difference	Total Misinvoicing
	(3-2)					(5-6)	(4+7)
(1)	(2)	(3)	(4)	(5)	(6)	(7)	(8)
1975	414	522	108	322	364	-42	66
1976	486	638	152	305	371	-66	86
1977	586	670	84	510	486	24	108
1978	558	619	61	638	673	-35	26
1979	575	778	203	797	969	-172	31
1980	591	734	143	1072	1229	-157	-14
1981	573	631	58	1370	1246	124	182
1982	611	672	61	1287	1416	-129	-68
1983	505	555	50	1338	1216	122	172
1984	698	767	69	1147	1043	104	173
1985	503	554	51	1275	1159	116	167
1986	512	650	138	1176	1386	-210	-72

1987	708	883	175	1447	1782	-335	-160
1988	852	1007	155	1637	1979	-342	-187
1989	1201	1148	-53	1704	2264	-560	-613
1990	1109	1427	318	1664	2237	-573	-255
1991	1137	1374	237	1186	1805	-619	-382
1992	1375	1513	138	1834	1660	174	312

Note: Column (4) indicates under-invoicing of exports, while column (7) over-invoicing of imports. The last column gives total of misinvoicing.

***Table 4.9:* Partner Country Data on Trade : India and Japan**

(Unit: U.S. dollar million)

Year	Indian Exports	Japan's Imports (3-2)	Difference	Indian Imports	Japan's Exports	Difference (5-6)	Total Mis-invoicing (4+7)
(1)	(2)	(3)	(4)	(5)	(6)	(7)	(8)
1975	450	658	208	514	471	43	251
1976	579	802	223	317	377	-60	163
1977	581	806	225	482	508	-26	199
1978	628	799	171	603	737	-134	37
1979	778	1044	266	658	774	-116	150
1980	924	1020	96	859	920	-61	35
1981	958	1053	95	1314	1195	119	214
1982	1018	1120	102	1376	1405	-29	73
1983	1028	1131	103	1577	1434	143	246
1984	1030	1133	103	1283	1166	117	220
1985	1089	1197	108	1770	1610	160	268
1986	1017	1309	292	1931	2119	-188	104

1987	1198	1546	348	1742	1977	-235	113
1988	1418	1806	388	1943	2083	-140	248
1989	2137	1963	-174	2217	2007	210	36
1990	1656	2075	419	1801	1711	90	509
1991	1654	2186	532	1364	1525	-161	371
1992	1850	2035	185	1637	1488	149	334

Note: Column (4) indicates under-invoicing of exports, while column (7) over-invoicing of imports.

Table 4.10: Partner Country Data on Trade: India and West Germany

(Unit: U.S. dollar million)

Year	Indian Exports (3-2)	Germany's Imports	Difference	Indian Imports	Germany's Exports	Difference (5-6)	Total Misinvoicing (4+7)
(1)	(2)	(3)	(4)	(5)	(6)	(7)	(8)
1975	130	196	66	452	354	98	164
1976	188	297	109	316	369	-53	56
1977	271	337	66	592	493	99	165
1978	305	381	76	703	639	64	140
1979	363	547	184	701	702	-1	183
1980	534	627	93	744	761	-17	76
1981	520	572	52	1096	996	100	152
1982	477	525	48	971	865	106	154
1983	448	492	44	915	832	83	127
1984	457	502	45	1014	922	92	137
1985	452	497	45	1268	1153	115	160
1986	525	648	123	1365	1567	-202	-79
1987	743	892	149	1583	1805	-222	-73

1988	900	1040	140	1804	1688	116	256
1989	1227	1217	-10	1707	1622	85	75
1990	1280	1581	301	1784	1730	54	355
1991	1271	1681	410	1551	1457	94	504
1992	1566	1723	157	1998	1816	182	339

Note: Column (4) indicates under-invoicing of exports, while column (7) over-invoicing of imports.

Table 4.11 : Partner Country Data on Trade: India and (former) U.S.S.R.

(Unit: U.S. dollar million)

Year	Indian Exports	U.S.S.R.. Imports (3-2)	Difference	Indian Imports	U.S.S.R. Exports	Differenece (5-6)	Total Misinvoicing (4+7)
(1)	(2)	(3)	(4)	(5)	(6)	(7)	(8)
1975	511	511	0	394	359	35	35
1976	476	476	0	235	214	21	21
1977	691	691	0	474	431	43	43
1978	564	564	0	472	429	43	43
1979	586	586	0	735	668	67	67
1980	608	648	40	999	926	73	113
1981	608	648	40	999	926	73	113
1982	1490	1639	149	1171	1064	107	256
1983	1490	1639	149	1171	1064	107	256
1984	1639	1803	164	1288	1171	117	281
1985	1721	1894	173	1352	1229	123	296
1986	1559	1715	156	698	635	63	219
1987	1380	1518	138	1211	1011	200	338

1988	1708	1878	170	1373	1248	125	295
1989	2398	2574	176	806	1052	-246	-70
1990	2868	3154	286	1322	1202	120	406
1991	1642	1806	164	520	472	48	212
1992	1806	1987	181	572	520	52	233

Note: Column (4) indicates under-invoicing of exports, while column (7) over-invoicing of imports.

Table 4.12: Partner Country Data on Trade : India and Hong Kong

(Unit: U.S. dollar million)

Year	Indian Exports	Hong Kong's Imports (3-2)	Difference	Indian Imports	Hong Kong's Exports	Difference (5-6)	Total Misinvoicing (4+7)
(1)	(2)	(3)	(4)	(5)	(6)	(7)	(8)
1975	34.1	37.7	3.6	1.9	3.1	-12	2.4
1976	76	92	16	3	7	-4	12
1977	77	88	11	8	12	-4	7
1978	126	115	-11	14	42	-28	-39
1979	119	117	-2	19	44	-25	-27
1980	126	165	39	29	53	-24	15
1981	120	132	12	69	63	6	18
1982	128	141	13	75	74	1	14
1983	148	162	14	90	82	8	22
1984	152	168	16	110	100	10	26
1985	149	164	15	135	123	12	27
1986	281	264	-17	63	160	-97	-114
1987	347	353	6	93	171	-78	-72

(1)	(2)	(3)	(4)	(5)	(6)	(7)	(8)
1988	456	505	49	105	237	-132	-83
1989	827	592	-235	316	279	37	-198
1990	545	595	50	158	305	-147	-97
1991	615	710	95	107	241	-134	-39
1992	685	753	68	363	330	33	101

Note : Column (4) indicates under-invoicing of exports, while column (7) over-invoicing of imports.

***Table 4.13:* Partner Country Data on Trade: India and Singapore**

(Unit: U.S . dollar million)

Year	Indian Exports (3-2)	Singapore's Imports	Difference	Indian Imports	Singapore's Exports	Difference (5-6)	Total Misinvoicing (4+7)
(1)	(2)	(3)	(4)	(5)	(6)	(7)	(8)
1975	33.4	57.5	24.1	11.8	41.5	-29.7	-5.6
1976	62	74	12	14	46	-32	-20
1977	78	78	0	32	143	-111	-111
1978	83	83	0	100	276	-176	-176
1979	98	101	3	110	226	-116	-113
1980	102	115	3	458	447	11	14
1981	121	133	12	624	568	56	68
1982	173	190	17	555	542	13	20
1983	317	348	31	481	438	43	74
1984	201	221	20	729	662	67	87
1985	201	221	20	534	485	49	69
1986	173	160	13	253	472	-219	-206
1987	188	250	62	310	557	247	-185

1988	223	265	42	356	737	-381	-339
1989	371	304	-67	834	936	-102	-169
1990	308	374	66	689	1103	-414	-348
1991	386	421	35	311	1004	-793	-758
1992	425	463	38	342	1105	-763	-725

Note : Column (4) indicates under-invoicing of exports, while column (7) over-invoicing of imports.

4. Capital Flight : Models And Estimation The movement of capital across the political boundary occurs when the residents in a country extend loan to or purchase the title of assets from, the resident of another country. From the principle of balance of payment accounting we see that current account surplus becomes equal to the capital outflow plus an increase in the international measures. Thus a capital exporter provides a corresponding flow of goods and services to the importer of capital unless it is simply drawing down its reserves. This is the flow of real capital corresponding to the flow of financial capital. The flow of real capital enters the national income accounts in the form of trade surplus, (X-M), where X, M are aggregate exports and imports of the country.

The standard macro economic equilibrium can be written as

$$Y = C + I + G + (X\text{-}M) \tag{4.1}$$

Where Y, C, I and G are aggregate income, consumption, investment and government expenditure respectively. As income, that is not consumed (Y-C) is either paid in taxes (T) or saved, the national income identity (4.1) can be interpreted as that the sum of sectoral financial savings, including the foreign sector, must equal zero, or

$$(I\text{-}S) + (G\text{-}T) + (X\text{-}M) = 0 \tag{4.2}$$

The excess of investment over savings is to be financed by the inflow of capital, government budget remaining balanced, which means an excess of imports or exports. Thus the flow of capital finances the imbalances between savings and investment by the transfer of real resources from one country to the other.

The received doctrine since the classical times is that capital would flow abroad only if it were attracted by a higher rate of return. Though early studies on the relative profitability of domestic and foreign investment of capital in Britain (Lehfeldt,

1913) and France (White, 1933) cast doubt on the premise that return on foreign investment of a unit of capital was consistently higher. It means that capital flows even if the return is not higher.

In the post-war period, the theories on balance of payment began to explain the international capital movement. Fleming (1962) and Mundell (1968) introduced the capital account into the macro-economic models of the open economy and they assumed that "a given differential in the interest rate between two countries would result in a given continuing capital flow". Later on this theory became known as flow theory of the capital account, as it gives a theoretical frame of the initial movement of capital induced by a difference in the real interest rate.

The portfolio theory as developed by Markowitz (1952) and Tobin (1958) argues that investors seek to distribute their stock of wealth among the available assets in such a way that utility becomes maximum. The latter depends on both expected returns and its variance, which implies that returns on most asset bear risk. Thus portfolio theory suggests that, if wealth were constant, a given interest rate differential would make an efficient distribution of the stock of capital. Thus any change in the relative interest rate would create a separate distribution of the stock of capital and the flow would stop. This is known as stock theory of capital account and its difference with the flow theory was highlighted by Branson (1968). The theory puts emphasis on the distribution of world assets (capital) depending on the interest differential among the countries.

But capital flow cannot stop across countries, as portfolio adjustment is not completed instantaneously but is spread out through time. The rate of adjustment is determined by transactions and recontracting costs, which may involve a long stretch of time. Further, in the case of perfect mobility of capital the flow and the stock theories of capital lose their differences as any country can borrow an unlimited amount of capital from the global capital market at the market rate of interest.

Leaving aside the documented part of the international transaction of capital, the latter move across the political boundaries through the smuggling of exports and imports of merchandise and currencies. Documentation apart, this sort of movement is largely guided by market forces like differentials in interest rate and taxes. Sometimes political instability induces large scale transfer of capital which may or may not be associated with large scale migration of population which are seen nowadays in the eastern Europe and Africa.

In a currency less world the difference between the export and import of goods and services is adjusted by the opposite movement of gold. In modern times gold has been substituted by the international currency, the U.S. dollar. But this has brought complication as the movement of dollar implies either the country is debtor or it is given loan to the partner country. In either case further adjustment with real goods is called for. This shows that international trade is a barter as Ricardo noted in the Principles (1817):

"Gold and silver having been chosen for the general medium of circulation, they are, by the competition of commerce, distributed in such proportions amongst the different countries of the world as to accommodate themselves to the natural traffic which would take place if no such metals existed, and the trade between countries were purely a trade of barter".

Keeping the above observations in mind we can write from (4.2)

$$(I\text{-}S) + (G\text{-}T) = (M\text{-}X) \qquad (4.3)$$

and the discrepancy in the private sector (I = S) and in the government sector (G = T) will be reflected in the non-zero solution to the right hand side of (4.3). Thus we can write the following identity.

$$X + Trf = M + r.\,B + Tr^{*} \qquad (4.4)$$

When Trf is the official transfer in the form of loan, r is the rate of interest on existing foreign debt B, this rB is the interest liability for foreign debt, and Tr^* is the private transfer to foreign land. Here the entries Trf, rB and Tr^* are all the items in the capital account of the balance of payments and Tr^* may or may not be documented and this is the quantum of capital flight if we assume that the country is not exporting capital officially in the form of foreign direct investment, otherwise another term will be added to the r.h.s. of equation (4.4).
from (4.4) again

$$Tr^* = (X-M) + (Trf - r.B) \quad (4.5)$$

or capital flight (Tr^*) depends on the surplus (or deficit) of the current account, the inflow of capital and the volume of foreign debt of the country.

What determines the volume of current account surplus or deficit? Since it is a gap between the export and import, the factors influencing the latter are important. Standard macro-economic theories suggest that gross domestic product (GDP), relative price (which is a ratio of domestic (P) to foreign price level (P^*) and exchange rate influence both the export and import of the country. Further, the real interest rate differential influences the capital inflow as well as the liability of the maintenance of foreign debt. Given that the institutional factors remain the same, the macro-economic variables influence the international flow of funds.

From the above discussion we can write the equation of the capital flight in a functional form and this is

$$Tr = F\,(GDP, P, P^*, ER, r, r^*, B)$$

Sometimes it is argued that it is not the absolute value of the exchange rate but rather the expected rate of depreciation of the currency which influences the quantum of capital flight. To capture this aspect the premium in the black market of the foreign currency (in the form of the ratio of black market exchange rate to the official rate) is taken as a proxy. Again, inflation in the domestic economy is a destabilizing force and it erodes the credibility of the currency. In the extreme situation higher rate of inflation induces a flight from the domestic currency, which is one form of capital flight. Thus instead of absolute price level, some studies emphasise rate of inflation as one of the determinant.

Several attempts are made in the literature to estimate the equation (4.6) in a variety of forms with changes in the explanatory variables. Cuddington (1987) has tried several forms keeping rate of inflation, exchange rate expectation, domestic and foreign interest rate, real exchange rate and disbursement of foreign loans. Both real exchange rate (indirect quotation) and volume of disbursement of loans have positive influence on capital flight, according to Cuddington. But Cuddington (1986) considers rate of inflation as an explanatory variable with positive influence on capital flight.

Boyce (1992) has used a model for the estimation of capital flight from Phili ppines which includes the level of country's foreign exchange reserve, apart from net debt disbursement and gross domestic product. Rob Vos (1992) has included the private saving rate and the rate of debt accumulation in his model for the estimation of capital flight from Phili ppines apart from other variables. Sometimes, political events or some important event in other countries are inserted into the model as dummies to capture the effects, if any.

In the present study two models are estimated and these are the following :

$$CF = F(\underset{+}{PREM},\ \underset{-}{RER},\ \underset{+}{INF},\ \underset{+}{GAP}) \quad (4.7) \quad \text{and}$$

$$CF/GDP = F(\underset{+}{PREM},\ \underset{-}{RER},\ \underset{+}{INF},\ \underset{+}{GAP}) \quad (4.8)$$

The premium in the black market of foreign currency defined as a ratio of the black market rate to the official rate of the exchange rate of Indian rupee (direct quotation e.g. the price of one U.S. dollar in terms of rupees) is one explanatory variable (PREM) in the function. If this premium goes up, the incentive becomes higher to encash foreign currency in the black market rather than in the official market. So the effect is positive, and we have put a plus sign (+) below.

The way we have defined the exchange rate, real exchange rate (RER) is derived by multiplying the nominal exchange rate with the ratio of foreign to domestic price level. Thus appreciation of the RER means lowering its value. So when RER declines i.e. real exchange rate appreciates, the overvalued position of the currency induces economic agents to shift their assets abroad so that these can be converted later at a more suitable exchange rate. So the relation between the capital flight and the real exchange rate is an inverse one and the expected sign is negative.

Inflation is an economically destablising force in an economy and if it becomes a persistent feature, the stability of the present exchange rate under a fixed exchange rate regime becomes doubtful. Thus if the inflation rate becomes higher, the inducement to shift capital abroad becomes stronger and the relation is direct. So the expected sign is positive.

Interest rate differential across countries has played an important part in the international adjustment of the portfolio. If the foreign interest is higher compared to the domestic rate, economic agents will shift their assets to foreign lands in the expectation of higher return, which is of course adjusted to the relative risks involved in placing funds outside the country. If we define GAP as the difference between the foreign interest rate and the domestic interest rate, then the relation between the gap and the volume of capital flight will be direct and the expected sign will be positive.

From the above discussion the expected sign of the coefficients of the independent variables in the estimable equation (4.7) can be written as :

$F_1 > 0, f_2 < 0, f_3 > 0$, and $f_4 > 0$

In case of equation (4.8), the relations hold as above.

Data, Methodology And Estimation The data on capital flight are based on our estimation of the same in Section 3. There are several estimates of capital flight, but only two–that of World Bank and of Cuddington-are taken for the purpose of the estimation of the models. The data on all other economic variables are collected from various issues of International Finance Statistics (IMF).

The period covered for estimation of the models is 1969-1989. The data of some economic variables prior to 1969 are not available and similar is the situation of the period after 1989. Data relate to annual time-series which may create problem for serial auto-correlation. For this the estimation of all the models are done by Cochrane-Orcutt method of estimation.

The unit of all data are in millions of U.S. dollars and official exchange rate of Indian rupee has been used for the conversion whenever necessary. The interest differential (GAP) is calculated by taking the difference of Indian interest rate (money market rate, MMR) from the lending rate of the U.S.A.

Another important thing is that all the regressions are based on the absolute values of the variables.

Empirical Results From Table 4.14 we find that the coefficient of the premium is not significant and it has a wrong sign too. But the coefficient of the RER is significant and with expected sign. The coefficient of inflation, having wrong sign, is significant at 17 per cent level only. The value of adjusted R^2 is 0.61 and that of D.W. statistic is 1.77 which gives the value of rho (the estimated value of serial correlation which stabilises after iterations done in Cochrane-Orcutt method) as 0.115.

One period lag has been introduced in the explanatory variables in Model 2 in table 4.14. While the coefficients of the lagged values are not significant, the coefficient of inflation (INF) has been significant with negative sign. It means that higher inflation at home has induced less capital flight contrary to existing norm in the literature. Is it due to the fact that higher domestic inflation is inducing agents to pour money in the lucrative sectors in the country like real estate? This aspect is an interesting point.

The third model takes lagged values of real exchange rate (RER) and the interest differential (GAP) as the only explanatory variable. While the coefficient of RER is positive and significant, that of GAP is negative and not significant. Probably the model is not correctly specified in its present form.

As if to remove the deficiency in model 3, we have estimated model 4 and we find that both the coefficients of RER and GAP are significant though the coefficient of GAP is negative, instead of being positive.

While Table 4.14 shows absolute value of capital flight as the dependent variable, in Table 4.15, the dependent variable is the ratio of capital flight to GDP. The estimation of model 1 (conforming to equation 4.8) shows that the intercept term and the coefficient of RER are significant and the latter is of expected sign. The value of adjusted R^2 is 0.58, that of D.W. statistic 1.81 with the value of rho as 0.1. In model 2 the lagged values of the dependent variable (CF/GDP) in introduced on the right hand side of the equation. We find that the coefficient of (CF/GDP) is positive and significant at 15 per cent level only, while the coefficient of RER in negative and significant. There is no significant change with the introduction of the lagged value of the dependent variable in model 2.

In Table 4.16, the absolute value of capital flight according to Cuddington definition has been taken. In model 1, the coefficient of a premium is positive, but not significant, while the coefficient of RER is negative as expected and it is significant. The coefficient of inflation (INF) is not significant. The value of adjusted R^2 is 0.47 while D.W. statistic is 1.75. In model 2, one period lag of the independent variables are introduced and this has changed the results to some extent. The coefficient of INF_t has been more meaningful (level of significance increases), though negative; but the coefficient of INF_{t-1} is positive, but not significant. In fact, the coefficients of lagged variables are not significant at all. Though the value of adjusted R^2 has improved.

One significant common result of all the models is that the real exchange rate has significant negative impact on the capital flight. This supports to the prevailing theoretical position that overvalued exchange rate induces capital flight. Even from the table we see that in the 80s the RER depreciated on an average and during this phase the value of capital flight has been negative.

Second, neither inflation, nor the premium in the black market of foreign currency has any significant effect on the capital flight from India. Perhaps, in a relative context, the inflation record of India is not so bad as to cause capital flight. The issue regarding the black market premium is puzzling.

Third, whether we take the dependent variable in absolute terms or in a ratio (Table 4.15), the dimension of the major results remain the same.

We have calculated the time-series of the misinvoicing in India's trade with seven major countries. Those figures are not used for any empirical estimation because the c.i.f./f.o.b. conversions have not been carried out. The reason for not doing so has been explained earlier. But because of this, those figures are kept for a qualitative judgement of the issue of capital flight from India. Of course, researchers use these discrepancies as the measure of capital flight from the developing countries (Gulati, 1987). Considering the importance of the seven countries taken in this study in the international trade with India, the time series of misinvoicing show that significant amount of capital flight takes place through this route. Further, the under-invoicing of imports in some cases shows the distortions due to high tariff regime in the country.

Another important issue in the capital flight question is whether past volume of capital flight influences the outflow of capital at present. To have the answer of this question the following regression has been estimated based on the Cuddington definition of capital flight (period 1970-1989:

$$\begin{aligned} CUDKF = {} & 718.21\ \underset{(1.30)}{PREM_t} - 117.4\ \underset{(-1.70)}{REP_t} \\ & + 2096.89\ \underset{(1.25)}{INF_t} + 0.706\ \underset{(2.99)}{CUDKF_{t-1}} + e \end{aligned}$$

Adjusted $R^2 = 0.48$
D.W. statistics = 1.85'
n = 20

We find that the coefficient of $CUDKF_{t-1}$ is positive and significant. This gives some justification to the contention that capital flight is dynamic in nature and past value of capital flight induces the flight of capital in the future. (Gibson and Tsakalotos, 1993).

***Table 4.14* : Capital Flight : Model Estimation**

Definition : World Bank

Dependent Variable : Capital Flight (CF)				
Independent Variables	Model 1	Model 2	Model 3	Model 4
Intercept	23883.81	26338.06	-11491.16	14922.68
	(3.08)**	(4.46)**	(-0.686)	(1.59)
Prem t	-2330.64	-4382.24		-1942.82
	(-0.78)	(-1.395)		(-0.72)
Prem t-1		-1441.21		
		(-0.456)		
RER t	-1095.98	-2389.23		-1278.70
	(3.51)**	(-3.187)**		(-2.00)**
RER t-1	838.51	1953.77		
		(0.96)	(3.15)**	
INF t	-11697.13	-21751.33		-4807.53
	(-1.425)	(-2.376)**	(-0.72)	
INF t-1		-8237.82		
		(- 0.917)		
GAP				-556.77**
				(-2.85)
GAP t-1			-243.31	
			(-1.29)	
Adjusted R^2	0.61	0.567	0.61	0.71
D W statistic	1.77	1.03	2.24	1.81
SEE	73805532	72054151	75206540	49222549
n	21	21	21	20

** Significant at 5 per cent level or lower.

Table 4.15 : Capital Flight : Model Estimation

Definition : World Bank (1970-1989)

Dependent Variable : Ratio of Capital Flight to GDP (CF/GDP)		
Independent Variables	Model 1	Model 2
Intercept	0.108 (2.688)	0.087 (2.24)
Prem t	-0.01 (-0.685)	-0.012 (-0.87)
INF t	- 0.05 (-1.177)	- 0.07 (-1.48)
RER t	-0.009 (-3.03)	-0.0062 (-2.457)
(CF/GDP) t-1		0.382 (1.538)*
Adjusted R^2	0.58	0.563
D W statistic	1.81	1.925
SEE	0.0018	0.0018
n	20	20

* Significant at 15 per cent level

Table 4.16 Capital Flight : Model Estimation : 1970-1989
(Definition : Cuddington)

Dependent Variable : Capital		Flight (CUDKF)
Independent Variables	Model 1	Mode l2
Intercept	3990.55	5725.34
	(2.02)*	(2.65)**
Prem t	213.8	-1386.64
	(0.28)	(-1.16)
INF t	-1362.10	-4662.52
	(-0.646)	(-1.69)
GAP t	17.91	-58.62
	(0.36)	(-0.90)
RER	-400.18	-502.29
	(2.83)**	(-2.55)**
INF t-1		1332.44
		(0.536)
RER t-1		132.68
		(0.572)
PREM t-1		114.72
		(0.14)
GAP t-1		166.62
		(1.90)
Adjusted R	0.47	0.66
D W statistics	1.75	1.86
SEE	4082496	3583607
n	20	20

* Significant at 6 per cent level
** Significant of 5 per cent level or less

When capital flight is seen as a portfolio adjustment problems of the rich individuals of the developing countries who want to evade the taxation net of the authority, the inflow and outflow of capital take place as the situation warrants. Thus a one-to-one correspondence is established between the flight of capital and the disbursement of loans (Phili ppines) or between capital flight and the size of the negative balance of trade (Mexico). In either case the past values of flight capital influences the present capital flight.

Capital flight from the developing countries is sometimes associated with medium or long-run capital movements. The latter creates confusion regarding the estimation of the flight. How to disentangle these two issues? One method of approaching this problem might be to start with a broader measure of capital flows (say, total capital flows minus foreign direct investment). We then regress this amount on the rates of return and a scale variable. The residuals are estimated and these are taken as measure of capital flight. Such measure of capital flight would treat the outflow as capital flow motivated by factors other than relative returns and wealth. But capital flight has also been defined outflow including the short-term speculative flows arising from differences in the rates of return. The latter may be caused by political instability and/or an instability in the exchange rate of the currency.

The empirical exercise have identified the determinants of capital flight in the case of India. It also tries to measure the strength of influence of these factors.The quantification of the influences of individual factor will help to identify the areas where policy change should get priority. This will help in the formulation of the policies to prevent the outflow of capital.

5. Conclusion India has been a relatively open society since 1950 though an elaborate system of exchange control and a near-ban on the movement of capital at the international level has always existed. But millions of Indians are living abroad and a significant percentage of them maintain close link with their motherland. This has resulted in a significant migration of Indian population to foreign lands–in Middle East, in Europe or in North America. The openness of the society is significant in the sense that a two-way flow has always been discernible in population. This sort of situation creates the potential of the outflow of capital and the so-called "havla transaction" in the Middle East is just one manifestation of this.

The flight of capital from India has not been uniform and in recent years we see negative capital flight. But this is as per World Bank and similar definition.This situation is quite comparable to the situations in other developing countries. The capital accumulated abroad enters into domestic economy in opportune moments and that sometimes inflates the prices of the real estate and of the shares. Again, as in the recent liberalisation environment, this sort of capital held abroad may enter into the economy in the guise of direct foreign investment. One should not bother about this so long the "cat kills the mice", as the Chinese proverb goes.

The analysis in the present study shows that the real exchange rate has significant influence on the flight of capital. The stability of the exchange rate of the domestic currency and the insignificant premium in the black market rate give the necessary signal to the economic agents who are holding their foreign earnings abroad in the expectation of further depreciation of the home currency in which case they are going to reap the gain. That the stability and/or a depreciation of the real exchange rate should have a significant impact on the capital flight is also revealed in the estimated result as the coefficient has the correct sign and it is significant.

It has been found that inflation and the premium of the black market rate of Indian rupee have no significant impact on the flight of capital from the country. There may be two explanations for this. First, inflation in India has been associated with lopsided price movement and price rise of the real estate and of the "white goods" are much more pronounced. It is possible that unofficial income, generated at home and abroad, has flowed into these areas. The prices ruling in these areas are difficult to justify by the "mean income level" of the country. The lesson is that fiscal policies should not mistreat the real estate or bond holders. In that case capital will move abroad.

Second, the openness of the society and an elite culture at the top coupled with the consumerism initiated in the 80s have given some socio-economic assurances to the agents that their capital is not at stake while invested at home in some areas. Though it has created distributional problem, it prevents capital flight also.

An undervalued currency, a good international reserve, a good record of debt servicing with a lower volume of international debt and a low rate of inflation are the factors that prevent the outflow of capital. Any country desirous of preventing the outflow of capital should maintain these characteristics while pursuing domestic, fiscal and monetary policies. India is no exception in this regard.

One interesting question is whether the developing countries, who are mostly the victims in capital flight, will be able to get back the capital. On this issue Morgan Guaranty (1986) argues:

LDC capital outflow have to be tackled as part of the solution to the debt problem, not as something that need be addressed only later. If capital flight is given a free ride in the cabooze of the LDC debt train, the train has little hope of making the station. It is both necessary and feasible to deal forthrightly with issues affecting capital flight. It is necessary for quantitative and psychological reasons; it is feasible because the causes of capital flight are fairly well understood, and the means exist to stem and reverse it.

The LDC countries should reform their economic system to get back some of the capital they have lost. Most important thing is the stoppage of the flight of capital and if they succeed in that the condition of these economies will improve.

Literature Cited Ashton, T.S. (1959), *Economic Fluctuations in England, 1700-1800,* Oxford, England, Clarendon Press.

Bhagawati, J.N. (1964) On the Underinvoicing of Imports, *Bulletin of the Oxford University Institute of Statistics,* November.

Bhagawati, J.N., A. Krueger and C Wibulswasdi, (1974), Capital Flight from LDCs : A Statistical Analysis, in Bhagawati (ed.), *Illegal Transactions in International Trade,* Amsterdam, North-Holland.

Bhandari, J.S. and B. Decaluwe, (1986), A Framework for the Analysis of legal and Fraudulent Trade Transaction in "Parallel" Exchange Market, *Weltwirtschaftliches Archiv*, Fasc 3.

Boyce, J.K. (1992), The Revolving Door? External Debt and Capital Flight : A Philippine Case Study, *World Development,* 20(3), March, 335-349

Branson, W.H. (1968), *Financial Capital Flows in the United States Balance of Payments,* Amsterdam; North-Holland.

Brown, B. (1987), *The Flight of International Capital : A Contemporary History,* London, Croom Helen.

Cline, W.R. (1986), Unpublished Estimates, as reported in Cumby and Levich (1987).

Cuddington, J.T. (1986), *Capital Flight : Estimates, Issues and*

Explanations, Princeton, Princeton University.

Cuddington, J.T. (1987), Macroeconomic Determinants of Capital Flight : An Econometric Investigation, in Lessard and Williamson (eds.). (1987).

Cumby, R. and R. Levich (1987), On the Definition and Magnitude of Recent Capital Flight, in Lessard and Williamson (eds.).

Diaz-Alejandro, C.F. (1984), Latin American Debt : I don't think we are in Kansas any more, *Brookings Papers on Economic Activity,* No. 2, pp. 335-389.

Dooley, M.P. (1986) Country Specific Risk Premiums, Capital Flight, and Net Investment Income Payments in Selected Developing Countries, *International Monetary Fund Departmental Memorandum* 86/17, Washington.

Dooley, M.P. W. Helkie; R. Tryon; and John Underwood (D-H-T-U), (1983), An Analysis of External Debt Positions of Eight Developing Countries Through 1990, *Journal of Development Economics,* May

Dornbusch, R. (1985), Budget Deficit, External Debt and Disequilibrium Exchange Rates, in *External Debt Problems of Developing Countries,* edited by G. Smith and J. Cuddington, Washington, World Bank.

Erbe, S. (1985), The flight of Capital from Developing Countries, *Inter-economics,* November-December, 268-75

Fleming, J.M. (1962), Domestic Financial Policies Under Fixed and Floating Exchange Rates, *IMF Staff Papers 9,* November, 369-79.

Gibson, H.D. and E. Tsakalotos (1993), Testing a Flow Model of Capital Flight in Five European Countries, *The Manchester School,* June, pp. 144-166.

Gulati, S.K. (1987), A Note on Trade Misinvoicing, in Lessard and Williamson (eds.).

Hawtrey, R.G. (1919), *Currency and Credit,* London, Longmans, Green.

Hector, G. (1985), Nervous Money Keeps on Fleeing, *Fortune, December 23.*

International Monetary Fund, *International Financial Statistics,* Various Issues, Washington D.C.

Kanitz, S.C. (1984), Renegotiating the Brazilian Debt, *Wall Street Journal,* September 21.

Khan, M.S. and N. U.L. Haque (1987), Capital Flight from Developing Countries, *Finance and Development,* IMF, 24, 2-5.

Kindleberger, C.P. (1987), A Historical Perspective, in Lessard and Williamson (eds).

Lehfeldt, R.A. (1913), The rate of interest on British and foreign investment, *Journal of the Royal Statistical Society,* January. 196-207 (also March 1913, March 1914 and May 1915 in parts)

Lessard D.R. and J. Williamson (1987), *Capital Flight and third world Debt,* Washington D.C., Institute for International Economics.

Markowitz H. (1952), Portfolio Selection, *Journal of Finance,* 7 March, 77-91

Morgan Guaranty Trust Co. (1986), LDC Capital Flight, *World Financial Market,* March, pp. 13-15

Mundell, R.A. (1968), *International Economics,* London, Macmillan.

Pinto, B. (1989), Black Market Premia, Exchange Rate Unification, and Inflation in Sub-Saharan Africa, *The World Bank Economic Review,* September 3, 321-338

Ricardo, D. (1817), *The Principle of Political Economy and Taxation,* London; J.M. Dent and Sons, 1911.

Tobin, J. (1958), Liquidity preference as behaviour towards risk, *Review of Economic Studies,* February 25, 65-86

Vos, R. (1992), Private Foreign Asset Accumulation, Not Just Capital Flight : Evidence from the Philippines, *The Journal of Development Studies,* April 28, pp. 500-537.

Walter I (1985), *Secret Money, London,* George Allen and Unwin.

While, H.D. (1933), *The French International Accounts 1880-1913,* Cambridge, Mass; Harvard Economic Studies.

World Bank (1985), *World Development Report 1985,* New York, Oxford University Press.

V

INTERNATIONAL RESERVE AND LIQUIDITY

[illegible] there have been considerable [illegible] about the desirability of holding a critical minimum level of international reserves on the part of a country to meet the import expenditure. What determines the critical level is altogether a different matter. [illegible] to ten months' import bill is taken [illegible] determination of that level. Among [illegible] today's economies [illegible] only the reserve of gold and foreign exchange [illegible] gives [illegible] to the [illegible] of general control [illegible] the economy.

In the [illegible] debate [illegible] about the [illegible] increase in international [illegible] was the [illegible] at the [illegible] level. Since U.S. dollar had [illegible] international currency through the Bretton Woods Agreement, the Federal Reserve

INTRODUCTION

People In General and the economists in particular have been conscious nowadays about the desirability of holding a critical minimum level of international reserve on the part of a country to meet the import expenditure. What determines the critical level is altogether a different matter, but six to ten months' import bill is taken as good measure for the determination of that level. Alternatively, in today's world of fiat money the reserve of gold and foreign exchange of a country gives some credibility to the currency of the country as people in general consider the level of international reserve as the amount of backing the currency enjoys.

In the 60s a debate arose about the imperative of increasing international liquidity and that was the concern at the global level. Since U.S. dollar had been the international currency through the Bretton Woods Agreement, the Federal Reserve of the U.S.A. agreed to bear the burden of providing necessary liquidity to the world trade and commerce. At that time Professor Triffin raised the interesting question of the ability of the world monetary systems to maintain sufficient liquidity for the smooth functioning of international trade and commerce. The interest in the study of the adequacy of the holding of international measure became important since then.

Definition According to Palgrave Dictionary of Economics international liquidity is considered as that stock of asset which is available to a country's monetary authorities to cover payments imbalances (when exchange rate is fixed) or to influence the exchange value of the currency (when the exchange rate is flexible).

The standard level of international reserve (IR) of a country consists of the following four elements:

(a) Gold

(b) Short term foreign exchange holding in convertible currencies

(c) Special drawing rights (SDR)

(d) Reserve position in International Monetary Fund (IMF)

If we see the elements it becomes clear that the level of international reserve can be considered as a stock of reserve which represents the purchasing power of the country as a whole and at the disposal of the monetary authority which can be used to moderate the domestic economic impact of the decline in foreign exchange recei pt.

The literature on the international reserve has explored varied aspects of the same and some of these are as follows:

First, with the growth of trade and commerce, volatility of the earnings of foreign exchange are rising and this necessitate the maintenance a minimum level of international reserve as a cushion to meet that sort of situation.

Second, there is a close parallel between the income elasticity of cash balance in the domestic money market and the income elasticity of holding IR.

Third, the changes in the level of IR may be independent of the movement of trade and the operation of international capital market can change the level of IR. When the currency of the country is fully convertible and *free* movement of capital is allowed, the level and significance of IR becomes sharply different compared to the case of a typical developing country with fixed exchange rate regime and restriction on the movement of capital.

We will explore the important factors which determine the adequacy of international reserve of a country in the following sections. The emphasis will be at the individual country level, and thus the debate of the desirability of maintaining adequate international liquidity has not been pursued here.The interested reader can see Kennen (1963) in this regard.

2. Review Of The Literature Since the late 50s many papers have been written on the theme of international reserve and these come under broadly two categories: the world reserve problem and how the International Monetary Fund would solve the problem of inadequate world level liquidity so that rising trade among the member countries is not adversely affected. The second channel of research continued regarding the optimal level of reserve from the standpoint of a single country. The latter problem has assumed importance in view of the floating exchange rate regime established after the collapse of the Bretton Woods Agreement in the early 70s. There are at least five reviews of the literature on the subject since 1960 and these are : Clower and Lipsey (1968), Niehans (1970), Salant (1970), Grubel (1971) and Williamson (1973).

Almost all the studies explain that countries hold international reserve so that they can meet sudden temporary excess demand for foreign exchange and/or to meet short run adjustment in balance of trade. The central banks often intervene in the foreign exchange market by selling/buying foreign exchange. International reserves are defined to be assets or credits which can be used directly for intervention or which can be converted into foreign exchange quickly and with certainty. In practice, it has been necessary to pick up arbitrary cut off point on such scale and define international reserve as assets which are acceptable at all times to foreign economic agents (Heller, 1966; Machlup, 1966). International Monetary Fund has to forward estimates of international reserve and these estimates have been widely used in literature for different purposes (Flanders,1971; Kelly, 1970; Clark, 1971).

A country can have international reserve at the macro level and also private liabilities towards foreign exchange. Some authors consider whether international reserve should be adjusted to such private liabilities literature, portfolio theory (Brown, 1964 ; Kenen and Yudin, 1967). In the monetary theory literature, portfolio theory and financial intermediation have been developed and these tools have been used to explain the movement of international reserve in Kane (1965). Such a framework has some relevance with the discussion in Machlup (1966) and the studies of reserve assets composition (Kennen, 1963; Hageman, 1969). The portfolio model employed in Hageman computed stock-adjustment equation for 11 major countries on quarterly data of the 1950s and early 1960 and the study found good evidence that adjustment was far from instantaneous.

Triffin (1960) first explained the dilemma of the gold-exchange standard in the sense that either liquidity would be progressively limited as the U.S.A. would try to reduce deficit, or a continuous deficit would lead to a deterioration in the United States reserve ratio, and in the process confidence in dollar would be undermined. The latter would provoke the attempt to convert dollar into gold in a big way which might give signal for the collapse of the system. The first part of the Triffin thesis provoked the literature on the demand for international reserve. Regarding the second part of the Triffin's thesis, this led to a discussion in the literature about the discretion of the member countries for the selection of their portfolio and its possible impact on the stability of the system (Gilbert, 1968; Mundell, 1968).

Mundell (1968) assumed that Europe's portfolio choice is determined by its views as to whether there should be an expansion of world income. When dollar is converted into gold in a big way, this sends a signal to the U.S.A. that income should contract and the latter is forced to restrict monetary expansion so as to restore its reserve ratio. Mundell prefers the United States to select a monetary policy appropriate to the requirement of the expansion of the world income and Europe should complement this by selecting a proper gold/dollar mix in the portfolio.

While IMF and the United States are the major suppliers of international reserve, some economists have developed a "demand-oriented theory" of supply (Johnson, 1964; Kindleberger, 1965; McKinnon,1967; Krause, 1970). According to this theory, the deficit of the United States is determined on the desire of the world regarding the accumulation of reserve and thus the deficit of the U.S.A. is the residual. If U.S.A. tries to reduce the deficit, the readjustment of policies of other countries would frustrate that effort. Thus some critical level of that deficit of the U.S.A. is not a measure of disequilibrium of the economy, but it is the result of "mutually-beneficial financial intermediation" among the nations. To some extent this readjustment procedure of the member countries is related theoretically what is known in the literature as the international quantity theory of money (IQTM). The basic assumption of the theory is that reserve changes influence monetary policies on gold standard lines and the monetary policies produce changes in the nominal income that reflects the price rather than quantity changes except in the very short run. On that basis one important conclusion of the theory is that the real level of reserve cannot be manipulated through the variation in the created nominal reserve because of the reactions of those affected with excess or deficient reserve holdings (Mundell, 1971).

The discussion on the issue of international reserve has attracted attention of the economist in the recent time. Thus Ben-Bassat and Gottlieb (1992) has analysed the quantum of optimal reserve and the probability of default risk. Also using simulation technique, optimum reserve (in case of Israel) has been calculated and then compared with actual reserve. The changes in the exchange rate regime can also affect the level of reserve (Heller and Khan, 1978). In another paper Ford and Huang (1994) has employed an ECM model for the computation of optimum reserve in China. One important conclusion of the paper is that reserve holding in China have maintained the long run relationship and a stable dynamic relationship with several economic parameters.

Exchange rate changes and the system should have some bearing on the growth of reserve which is explored in Frenkel (1978), while Frenkel (1989) has attempted to explain the problem of international liquidity and monetary control. Also a probabilistic framework has been attempted in the explanation of the growth changes in international reserve in Frenkel and Jovanovic (1981) and Hamada and Ueda (1977). Recently, the stability of the demand for international reserve has been discussed in Landell-Mills (1989) and Lizondo and Mathieson (1987). Also Edwards (1984) has explained the dynamic relationship between foreign borrowing, foreign debt and the level of reserve.

Adequacy Of Reserves And Demand For Reserve

There is a close parallel between the traditional demand for cash balances (explained by QTM) and the demand for reserve. The theory postulates a stable relationship in the demand for cash balance. If aggregate levels of imports is the measure of the total international transactions, a stable relationship can be postulated between the demand for international reserve and the volume of imports. The IMF report of 1953 and 1958 on international liquidity have stressed the importance of imports/ reserve ratio as a rough indicator of the adequacy of reserve (IMF, 1953, 1958). The reserve/import ratio has its limitation also (Niehans 1970). Also it has been pointed out by Heller (1968) that during the period 1951-66 when the aggregate reserve/import ratio of the world declined, the ratio of foreign exchange holdings of commercial banks to imports increased, (Heller, 1968). International reserve can be considered as a buffer stock of the medium of exchanges and the relationship between the two is much less tight compared to the relation between medium of exchange and transaction. This defect is sought to be corrected by W. M. Brown (1964) by relating reserve to the net external balance of the country. His analysis points to the importance to the analysis of the disturbances which can be the changes in the net external balance (Brown, 1964).

Reserve And Money Supply Nexus Instead of imports Scitovsky (1988) and Johnson (1988) relate adequacy of reserve with the premium that a reduction in reserve is equivalent to an excess of aggregate expenditure over receipts. Such excess expenditure means a reduction in cash balance. Thus BOP deficits and reserve losses should be interpreted essentially as a monetary phenomena. The Scitovsky argument can be put as follows :

The individual should be able to do collectively what they think they can do individually. The implication of this can be explained with the help of a Keynesian type trade model. In equilibrium, aggregate income Y must be equal to domestic demand plus export demand, which is treated as exogenous. If q is taken as the fraction which determines the domestic demand (both aggregate consumption and investment taken together), we can write the aggregate income in the following way:

$$Y = A + qY + X \quad \ldots\ldots\ldots\ldots\ldots\ldots (1) \quad A \text{ is constant}$$

Again, import is a function of income Y, or

$$M = B + mY \quad \ldots\ldots\ldots\ldots\ldots\ldots (2), \quad B \text{ is constant.}$$

If there is change in A and B, import will change. If export is not exogenous, this change will depend on the reaction of export. But assuming the latter exogenous, we get

$$dM = (m/(1-q))\, dA + dB \quad \ldots\ldots\ldots\ldots (3)$$

Scitovsky then postulates that the shifts in dA and dB are identified with desired spending out of cash balance dL. Clearly the cash balance dL of Professor Scitovsky is the international reserve of the country which gives the necessary liquidity to the country to buy commodities in the international market. Every monetary unit of that spending is assumed to be distributed between domestic goods and imports in the same way as marginal income dollars. Thus we get

$$dA = q/(m+q)\ dL, \quad \text{and} \quad \ldots\ldots (4)$$
$$dB = m/(m+q)\ dL \quad \ldots\ldots (5)$$

By substitution from (3), (4) and (5)

$$dM = (m/1-q)\left(\frac{q}{m+q}\right) dL + \left(\frac{m}{m+q}\right) dL$$

$$= dL\left(\frac{q}{m+q}\right)\left\{\frac{m}{1-q} + m/q\right\}$$

$$= dL\left(\frac{q\,m}{m+q}\right)\left(\frac{1}{q(1-q)}\right)$$

or

$$\frac{dM}{dL} = \left(\frac{q\,m}{m+q}\right)\left(\frac{1}{q(1-q)}\right) \quad \text{........ (6)}$$

Thus for exogenous exports, equation (6) gives the desirable minimum ratio of external reserve to domestic money supply. But Scitovsky's analysis shows that the ratio is subject to change for changes in m and q. Nonetheless, this analysis puts emphasis on the important relationship between external reserve and domestic money supply. Though the domestic money supply is not backed by gold, every central bank keeps the promise of converting domestic currency into foreign currency at fixed rate when demanded. This makes it imperative that central bank keeps a minimum international reserve as a backing to the currency in circulation with the public apart from the requirement of maintaining international liquidity.

The analysis of Scitovsky can also be extended to the macro-economic analysis (Niehans, 1970). Sometimes, the relation between level and growth of international reserve is emphasised (J.M. Fleming, 1967). He postulates that social welfare depends positively both on the level and growth of reserve.

Also Triffin (1960), Machlup (1967) and Gilbert (1968) have assembled huge evidence to show that the proportion to total reserve to aggregates like imports, money supply and liabilities of central bank cannot be expected to reveal simple regularities.

An early attempt to determine the need for international reserve and even to measure it is available in Marquez (1970), who also postulates that the need for reserve on the part of developing countries is much greater compared to the developed world, when the fixed exchange rate regime prevails. But Marquez opines that in the process of creating international reserve the countries are required to demonetise gold. This point refers to the analysis of Triffin (1960). As Patel (1970) mentions, if the possibility of gold revaluation were kept alive, there would always be pressure for countries not to use gold holdings, and gold would be frozen, and the need for other reserve would increase.

The argument that the developing countries have greater need for holding and maintaining international reserve for a number of reasons (instability in price of raw materials, instability of balance of payments etc.) is well established in the literature. Also factors like rigidities introduced by debt payments, volatility in the prices of primary factors in trade, and the inability of the poorer countries to attract short-term capital inflow, all these justify the greater need for maintaining higher reserve for the developing countries.

Reasons For Holding Reserve Though in normal circumstance a country should hold a certain amount of reserve, the holding of it is not costless. The opportunity cost of holding reserve is the differential income the country is to forego, which is the difference between the productivity of capital when invested domestically and the interest earned through the holding of the reserve. Still, there are important reasons why reserve should be held. At least three reasons are cited in the literature.

First, holding of reserve gives credibility to the monetary authority regarding financial strength. A visible strong financial position will prevent flight from the currency, whether it be by residents or non-resident creditors who might otherwise be tempted to sell a currency short. Further, a national "fiat" currency should be backed, at least partially, so that monetary authority remains ready to keep the promise of converting the liquidity liabilities (currency) into foreign exchange when desired. Also a large reserve enables the country to borrow foreign capital and enhance the liquidity by a multiplier if the country faces the possibility of capital flight.

Second, a certain level of reserve of the country can be used against "the contingency that the country may some day want to absorb resources from the rest of the world at a time when it cannot borrow or liquidate other foreign asset" (Cooper, 1970). These reasons for holding reserve refer to exceptional circumstances when normal internal or external economic relationship come to the point of breakdown.

Third, international reserve can be used to meet payments imbalances–something like those that are reversible or those that are once-for-all. The first type may come from seasonal patterns in payments, or from cyclical development in the economy. When alternative means of financing imbalances are costly or not easily available, while adjustment is needed, use of international reserve in the short run is preferable.

Monetarist Controversies And Reserve

A Macro-World View Two controversies in monetary theory are related to the question of international reserve. First is the question whether financial intermediation destroys the possibility of central bank control. Second is whether prices can be taken as autonomous so that variations in the nominal quantity of money imply variations in the real quantity of money, or whether prices in the long run adjust so as to make real balances correspond to what holders of money would demand.

The first question is related to the issue that whether it is justified if one assumes that the global nominal quantity of reserve can be controlled through the control of the issue of SDR.

The second question is related to the issue whether one is justified in the assumption that, even if the nominal aggregate of reserve can be controlled, such control will regulate the real quantity of international money.

Regarding the first question Johnson (Comment on Cooper's Paper, 1970) is of the view that the essence of the concepts of reserve needs is that the international monetary system rests on an ultimate reserve money in the international payments system and that is the special drawing rights (SDR). In the national monetary system this is a fact and this leads to the conclusion that financial intermediation cannot frustrate central bank control, because the intermediaries themselves require reserves and the latter constitute a demand for the ultimate reserve money. This becomes a fact in the international monetary system if monetary policy in the U.S.A. is constrained by the same need to maintain adequate reserves like any other country. But if such constraints are not there, and other countries are obliged to hold dollars, the U.S.A. effectively controls the nominal quantity of world reserves.

Regarding the second question the theoretical answer is simple and this is as such : the economic agents will vary the price level so as to reduce any given nominal quantity of money into the real quantity they desire. But when it comes to the policy level, it becomes an empirical question, which is whether within the time span permissible under policy plan, changes in the nominal reserve have effects on the quantity of real reserve or on prices. The implication of this empirical issue is much more complex. According to the theoretical assumption, price movements adjust real reserves to the desired level in the long run. According to this, there cannot be any shortage of international reserve. But facts speak otherwise and countries who hold reserves at a considerable level to prevent the undesirable consequences do so at a cost, as explained earlier.

When there is an increase in the level of international reserve in a country due to a mix of fiscal and monetary policies, it will affect other parameters of the economy in a pattern which are expected to follow a pattern quite predictable by the theory. Such a thing can be put up in a schematic form following Rhomberg (1970). This is shown in the following table.

Table 5.1: Possible effects of a Rise in Reserves on a Country's Policies

Description of policy change	effect on domestic demand (increase +; decrease –)
1. Reduce level of international liquidity (swaps, fund quotas)	0
2. Increase foreign aid grants	+
3. Untie foreign aid	–
4. Relax restrictions on capital exports or tighten restrictions on capital imports	(–)*
5. Relax restrictions on imports of goods and services	–
6. Reduce tariffs and import equalization taxes or reduce export subsidies and border tax rebates	–
7. Revalue exchange rate	–
8. Reduce interest rate or level of credit restraint and offset employment effect through fiscal policies	0
9. Expand domestic demand for goods and services	+

Source : R. R. Rhomberg (1970).
Estimation of effects of changes in international reserve, p. 176.

* The effect is uncertain though. The relaxation on restriction on capital exports is likely to increase interest rate and therefore have a negative effect on demand. But an increase in capital exports may facilitate an increase in exports in merchandise and this leads to the net effect somewhat ambiguous.

3. Theory, Model And Estimation The literature on the demand for international reserve has developed broadly on two complementary traditions. One tradition develops general equilibrium cost-benefit models and the estimating equation is derived from it (Kelly, 1970; Frenkel and Jovanovic, 1981; Ben-Bassort and Gottlieb, 1992). The second tradition is purely empirical (Frenkel, 1974, 1978; Heller and Khan, 1978; Edwards, 1983, 1984).

While every country maintains a decent level of international reserve, the dynamic behaviour of international reserve has been explained in literature in two alternative ways. One school has postulated that the movement of reserve responds to discrepancies between the desired reserve and the actual reserve held by the country (Clark, 1970; Iyoha, 1976; Heller and Khan, 1978; Bilson and Frenkel, 1979; Edwards, 1983). The second school offers an explanation through a simplified version of the monetary approach to the balance of payments. This school postulates that changes in the international reserve will be functionally related to the disequilibrium in the domestic money market. That is, international reserve will increase if there exists an excess demand for money, given the constant domestic credit; and again, international reserve will decrease if there exists an excess supply of money. In this sense, monetary approach implies that international reserve is a residual (Frenkel and Johnson, 1976). In a fixed exchange rate system, if actual reserve is less than the desired one, other things being given, the actual reserve will tend to rise and in order to make it feasible, there will be a tendency to reduce domestic credit. Again the possible simultaneity between the determination of the international reserve and the domestic credit has been explored in Genberg (1976).

The Model Following standard literature (McDonald, 1982; Archibald and Richmond, 1971; Ben-Bassat and Gottlieb, 1992):

a simple model for the demand for international reserve can be constructed in the following way :

The cost of the depletion of international reserve comes from the effects of the reduction of imports on the domestic product. The form is needed to restore the level of international reserve. If the ratio of imports to gross domestic product (m) is taken as the openness of the economy, a higher value of the openness (m) means the effect of import cut on the gross domestic product (GDP) will be less severe. This means that the cost is inversely related to the size of m. As cost is reflected in the loss of GDP, it can be written as

$$Co/Y = f1\ (m) \qquad \ldots\ldots \quad (1)$$

Again, holding international reserve is not costless. The opportunity cost of holding reserve depends on the difference between the economy's marginal productivity of capital (h) and the interest on the level of reserve (i). If r = (h-i), then the cost of reserve holding can be written as

$$C_1 = r\,R \qquad \ldots\ldots \quad (2)$$

Where R is the level of international reserve. Without loss of generality it can be assumed that productivity of capital at home will be higher than the borrowing cost mainly because of the existence of controls on international capital movement.

In the backdrop of the above two types of cost (of depletion and of holding), central bank of the country is to hold a certain amount of international reserve. Thus the total expected cost consists of two parts: (i) first foregone earnings C_1 in the case of positive reserve (quantified by the difference between h and i) and (ii) the social cost of the depletion of reserve Co. Thus we get

$$EC = w\,Co + (1 - w)\ C1 \qquad \ldots\ldots \quad (3)$$

Where w is the probability of reserve depletion and (1 - w) is the probability of reserve being positive.

Sovereign Risk Since a sudden depletion of international reserve reduces the lender's confidence about the financial viability of the country, the risk of reserve depletion is taken as same as the sovereign risk. Further, the probability of the depletion of the reserve depends on some economic factors like the ratio of reserve to imports (R/M), ratio of exports to imports (X/M), ratio of debt service to exports (D/X), and some other macro-economic factors (a catch all variable Z). We can write

$$w = f\ (R/M, X/M, D/X, Z) \qquad \ldots\ldots \qquad (4)$$

An increase in reserve ratio (R/M) will reduce the risk of default (sovereign risk), an increase in the ratio X/M will again reduce, but an increase in debt service ratio (D/X) will increase the default risk.

Rational Behaviour Of The Central Bank It can be postulated that the central bank will minimise the expected cost of holding international reserve with respect to the level of reserve.

The wealth constraint of the economy as a whole can be written as

$$K+A+R = W + DB \qquad \ldots\ldots \qquad (5)$$

Where K = aggregate capital stock of the economy
R = level of international reserve
A = other assets of the economy
W = net wealth and
DB = gross external debt

Further, (5) can be written as

$$DB = K + A + R - W \quad ..... \quad (6)$$

Which implies that gross external debt is endogeneous.

Substituting (1) and (2) into (3) we get the objective function as

$$\underset{(R)}{\text{Minimise}}\ EC = w\, Co\ (m,y) + (1 - w)\ r\ R..... \quad (7)$$

Subject to

$$w = (R/M, X/M, D/X, Z) \quad ..... \quad (8)$$

and also the wealth constraint (5).

The first and the second order condition for the optimisation process are

$$\frac{d\,EC}{dR} = 0 = \frac{dw}{dR} C_o\ (m, y) + w \frac{dC_o\ (m1,y)}{dR} + (1 - w)r \quad ..... \quad (9)$$

and

$$\frac{d^2EC}{dR^2} = EC_{RR} > 0 \quad ..... \quad (10)$$

Assuming that second order condition holds, the solution to the first order condition (9) can give the optimum level of reserve as

$$R^* = f\ (\ Co, y, r, X/M, D/x, Z) \quad ..... \quad (11)$$

Assuming that the function (11) is separable and additive, the optimum level of reserve is determined by the cost of reserve depletion, rate of interest and other economic variables.

It is clear from (11) that international reserve depends on gross domestic product, rate of interest, the ratio of exports over imports, the ratio of debt burden to exports and a scale variable. For the purpose of estimation we can take a proxy like the ratio of imports to GDP in place of the debt-export ratio. Further, the interest rate variable is dropped. Thus, in the modified form the equilibrium demand for international reserve can be written as

$$R = F \ (GDP, M/Y, X/M) \quad .... \quad (12)$$

and in linear logarithmic term it becomes

$$\ln R = bo + b1 \ln \ GDP + b2 \ \ln \ (M/Y) + b3 \ln (X/M) + U \quad .... \quad (13)$$

Where U is assumed to be stochastic and it obeys all the necessary properties. The time series estimation of the model is given below. The expected sign of the coefficients are :

b1 > 0, b2 > 0 and b3 > 0.

Table 5.2: Empirical estimation : Model 1.

Model 1 : ln R = bo + b1 ln GDP + b2 ln(M/Y) + b3 ln (X/M) +u

	Coefficients and statistics					adjusted		
Countries	bo	b1	b2	b3	DW	R^2	SEE	n
1. India	3.496	0.60	0.77	1.31	1.54	0.879	3.03	28
1966-1993	(0.445)	(1.01)	(1.12)	(1.83)				
2. USA	-6.694	1.16	-0.78	-0.548	1.54	0.81	2.3	24
1971-1994	(-3.03)	(9.90)	(-0.998)	(-0.534)				
3. Japan	-0.535	0.63	-0.859	0.069	1.4	0.937	0.69	24
1971-1994	(-0.684)	(9.16)	(-4.10)	(0.806)				
4. Portugal	-12.86	2.22	1.351	2.50	1.56	0.9	2.99	22
1971-1992	(-1.89)	(3.61)	(1.405)	(2.62)				
5. Spain	-5.98	1.22	-0.414	0.188	1.43	0.95	0.76	24
1971-1994	(-2.42)	(8.10)	(-0.862)	(0.370)				
6. France	4.56	0.69	2.39	0.289	2.09	0.44	3.78	23
1972-1994	(0.904)	(2.654)	(1.594)	(0.10)				

Note : Figures in parentheses are t-statistic

Estimation Of Time Series Model Model 1 Model 1 has been estimated with the data of six countries including India. Other countries are U.S.A., Japan, Portugal, Spain and France.

One significant aspect of the econometric result has been that the estimated coefficient of logarithm of GDP in all cases are positive and significant. But in cases of average propensity to import and the ratio of exports to imports, the estimated coefficients have not been in accordance to the theoretical expectation. In cases of India and France, the coefficients have been all positive as expected, but not statistically significant at 5 per cent level.

In all cases the estimation has been done by Cochrane - Orcutt method of estimation to take care of possible autocorrelation in the time series data. Also the data of the relevant economic variables of all the countries are collected from International Financial Statistics (IMF) and these are placed in the Appendix at the end of this chapter.This is done to maintain the continuity of the discussion.

Model 2 As noted in previous section the maintenance of a critical level of international reserve on the part of a country is necessitated mainly for two purposes–to meet short-run adjustments in the deficit of the current account and to maintain stability in the exchange rate in the floating exchange rate world. Regarding the first objective it is obvious that the changes in the exports and imports of the country causing changes in the current account will trigger changes in the level of international reserve. Thus forces which work behind the movements of the exports and imports influence the size and changes of the international reserves. In this connection two economic parameters can be mentioned and these are the gross domestic product of the country and the ratio of domestic price level to foreign price level.

An increase in the gross domestic product will increase the level of imports as absorption capacity of the economy increases and marginal propensity to import is positive. So far as exports are concerned, an increase in gross domestic product (GDP) will increase the supply of commodities in general and that facilitates exports expansion. Since an increase in imports increases the probability of deficit in current account which is to be met by drawing down the reserve, the expansion of income at home has negative effect on reserve through import expansion. But simultaneously, the expansion of exports will help building up of the reserve. Thus the effects of the expansion of GDP on the level of reserve is uncertain.

The inflation differential of a particular country affects its competitive power in the international trade. Thus, if domestic inflation rate is higher compared to inflation of the foreign country, the exports of the country suffers while imports increase, which leads to a depletion of the international reserve. Thus a change in the ratio (Pd/Pf), Pd being the price level of the domestic country and Pf the foreign country, will negatively affect the level and change of the reserves.

The level of international reserve also depends on the capital inflow and/or outflow and these are largely determined by the interest differential of the countries. If the domestic interest rate (r_d) is higher compared to the foreign interest rate (r_f), then capital inflow will take place, which helps build up the reserves. In general if we take the ratio (r_d/r_f), an increase in the ratio implies that domestic interest rate rising faster than foreign interest rate and this will facilitate the capital inflow and as a result international reserve will increase. Thus the effect of the interest rate is positive on the movement of reserve.

On the basis of the theoretical discussion above we can write the equation depicting the movement of reserve.

$$R = F\ (Y,\ P_d/P_f,\ r_d/r_f) \qquad .....(14)$$

Where Y is gross domestic product.

The function in linear estimable form can be written as

$$R_t = ao + a1.Y_t + a2\ (P_d/P_F)_t + a3\ (r_d/r_f)_t + u_t \quad .... \quad (15)$$

Where u_t is the stochastic error term, which is normally distributed and follows usual assumptions. The expected signs of the coefficients are : $a1 > o$; $a2 < o$; $a3 > o$
Two other estimable models in linear forms can be written from the above discussions. The change in reserves depends on the same set of variables as explained in (2), or

$$(R_t - R_{t-1}) = bo + b1\ Y_t + b2\ (Pd/Pf)_t + b3\ (rd/rf)_t + u_t \ ..... \quad (16)$$

Where u_t is the stochastic error terms and it follows normality and other usual assumptions. The expected sign of the coefficients should follow (2).

In the flexible exchange rate regime a significant level of international reserve should have a strengthening effect on the exchange rate, which is often seen in the international level. Thus exchange rate movement partly depends on the level of the reserve. To examine this hypothesis a model of the form

$$E = Co + C_1 R + u_2 \quad .....4$$

Can be constructed and estimated with $c_1 < 0$.

If we take the direct quote in the exchange rate, it means the units of domestic currency per unit foreign currency, i.e., U.S. dollar. In this an increase in the level of E means depreciation of the currency. Now when international reserve increases, beyond a point it creates pressure of appreciation on the exchange rate and thus the expected sign of the coefficient C_1 should be negative. This result is expected when other fundamentals of the economy remain unchanged.

Table 5.3: Estimation of the Model 2

Model : $R_t = ao + a1\,Y_t + a2(Pd/Pf)_t + a3(rd/rf)_t + u_t$

Countries	Coefficients and statistics ao	a1	a2	a3	DW	Adjusted R^2	SEE
1. India	81833.12	-0.0017	-2713.13	3.414	1.56	0.93	0403132
1960-1988	(0.217)	(-0.786)	(-1.095)	(3.65)			
2. Canada	-30678.17	0.0778	760.17	1.578	0.88	0.64	9019107
1960-1989	(-0.737)	(1.907)*	(0.031)	(1.76)			
3. Mexico	-2990.46	0.0001	2103.66	5.719	1.84	0.78	5674988
1960-1989	(-2.97)	(3.98)	(3.21)	(2.52)			
4. Singapore	-3291.41	0.398	-501.416	0.287	2.01	0.98	9125822
1960-1989	(-0.845)	(6.60)	(-0.220)	(0.303)			
5. Turkey	-555.37	0.000052	337.14	2.278	2.03	0.95	519029
1960-1988	(-4.129)	(6.47)	(4.12)	(9.42)			

6. Yugoslavia 1960-1988	-940.44 (-4.48)	1.575 (6.634)	82.166 (2.596)	3.378 (6.10)	1.46	0.81	2433372
7. United Kingdom 1960-1988	-74.415 (-2.195)	0.00023 (2.165)	13.98 (0.418)	3.318 (3.014)	2.02	0.83	487.6
8. Greece 1960-1988	-1924.85 (-1.064)	0.00040 (1.06)	2279.43 (1.59)	2.316 (2.116)	0.78	0.87	1790128
9. Pakistan 1960-1988	-1136.26 (-1.7.34)*	0.001 (0.653)	1171.70 (1.066)	4.40 (2.62)	2.02	0.5	1673650
10. Spain 1960-1989	-101729.36 (-1.593)	0.0036 (3.07)	8779.6 (0.3617)	3.29 (2.40)	1.54	0.9	162000000
11. Korea 1960-1989	-20530.45 (-0.653)	0.00019 (1.13)	8194.4 (0.679)	8.05 (2.23)	1.5	0.83	40311051

Note : Figures in parentheses are t-statistic

Table 5.4 : Estimation of the Model: Model 3

Model : R = ao + a1 Y + a2(Pd/Pf) + a3(rd/rf) +u2

Coefficients and statistics							
Countries	ao	a1	a2	a3	DW	R^2	SEE
1. India	-605.25	-0.00057	1128.05	2.424	1.52	0.39	0104995
1960-1988	(-0.314)	(-0.965)	(0.469)	(2.344)			
2. Canada	-18387.79	0.051	-2894.9	0.724	1.78	0.54	3236705
1960-1989	(-0.66)	(1.72)*	(-0.16)	(1.035)			
3. Mexico	-1205.94	0.000022	-11.60	3.24	2.34	0.5	0748360
1960-1989	(-1.324)	(1.073)	(-0.017)	(1.36)			
4. Singapore	29.328	0.037	-194.86	0.085	2.24	0.67	3335706
1960-1989	(0.024)	(3.132)	(-0.248)	(0.298)			
5. Turkey	103.786	-0.000014	319.13	1.082	2	0.26	1721576
1960-1988	(0.446)	(-1.02)	(2.23)	(2.78)			

6. Yugoslavia 1960-1988	151.09 (0.764)	-0.378 (-1.64)	114.56 (2.89)	1.429 (2.53)	2.19	0.35	4055078
7. United Kingdom 1960-1988	-16.955 (-1.57)	0.000082 (1.10)	-10.27 (-0.59)	1.488 (1.099)	1.996	0.047	735.93
8. Greece 1960-1988	-380.55 (-1.434)	-0.0001 (-1.157)	1165.27 (4.34)	2.65 (3.52)	1.88	0.67	803655
9. Pakistan 1960-1988	-175.87 (-0.469)	-0.00036 (-0.451)	298.44 (0.54)	0.728 (0.551)	2.07	-0.01	2520672
10. Spain 1960-1989	-291.86 (-0.077)	-0.00057 (-1.50)	18707.92 (2.305)	3.514 (2.26)	1.92	0.337	830000001
11. Korea 1960-1989	-228.27 (-0.209)	0.000086 (2.93)	-6398.03 (-2.34)	5.206 (1.92)	1.64	0.47	31292106

Note : Figures in parentheses are t-statistic

Table 5.5: Estimation of the Model: Model 4

Model : E = co + c1 R + u2

Coefficients and statistics Countries	co	c1	DW	SEE	Adjusted R^2
1. India 1960-1988	70.225 (0.359)	-0.00037 (-2.0895)	2.1	15.19	0.91
2. Mexico 1960-1989	19.666 (2.92)	-0.0022 (-0.689)	1.37	30873.12	0.96
3. Singapore 1960-1989	2.706 (6.71)	-0.0000513 (-2.36)	1.4	0.2278	0.95
4. Turkey 1960-1988	14.979 (0.546)	0.01 (0.397)	1.53	107771	0.97
5. Yugoslavia 1960-1988	0.0015 (0.802)	0.0000028 (1.69)*	0.83	0.01	0.95
6. United Kingdom 1960-1988	-2.057 (-0.257)	0.023 (3.955)	1.79	0.649	0.87
7. Greece 1960-1988	290.447 (0.38)	-0.0041 (-0.524)	0.83	0.93	2745.6
8. Pakistan 1960-1988	31.92 (0.618)	-0.00027 (-0.316)	1.98	55.98	0.913
9. Spain 1960-1989	820.83 (0.238)	-0.0018 (-2.48)	1.07	3299.26	0.88
10. Korea 1960-1989	1737.5 (1.05)	-0.016 (-2.86)	1.9	42008.7	0.94

Note : Figures in parentheses are t-statistic

Analysis Of The Estimation Of Model 2, Model 3 And Model 4. As reported earlier, the expected sign of estimated value of a1 may go either way. We find from Table 5.3, that for most countries the sign has been positive and also significant. In case of India it is not significant. The expected value of a2 should be negative and this is satisfied for almost all cases with good level of statistical significance. Thus the interest differential has a significant role to play in the explanation of the movement of international reserve.

In all 11 countries time series data are used for the estimation. To take care of possible autocorrelation problem all estimations are done by Cochrane-Orcutt method of estimation.

The estimation of Model 3 is different in the sense that the dependent variable is the first difference of the international reserve. The results of the estimation are not strikingly different.

Table 5.5 gives the results of the empirical estimation of model 4, which shows the exchange rate dependent on the level of international reserve. Theoretical expectation is that the sign of the estimated coefficient will be negative. From Table 5.5 we find that in seven cases out of 10 countries, the sign of the coefficient c1 is negative. But in case of India, Singapore, Spain and Korea, the sign is negative and significant. We have got positive result in case of three countries, United Kingdom, Yugoslavia and Turkey and of these three cases, the coefficient of United Kingdom is significant. The estimation in all cases are done by Cochrane-Orcutt method of estimation.

Estimation Of Cross-Section The Model The empirical estimation of the model has been done with a cross-section sample of 15 countries for two years, 1984 and 1989. The countries are :

India, Japan, Australia, New Zealand, Indonesia, Malaysia, Thailand, Turkey, Egypt, Algeria, Sri Lanka, Hungary, Denmark, Belgium and Iran.

The results are as follows (INTR is international reserve, other symbols are as explained earlier).

For the year 1984

$$\ln INTR = \underset{(2.08)}{3.418} + \underset{(2.74)}{0.455} \ln GDP + 0.10 \ln (M/Y) + \underset{(0.42)}{0.055} \ln (X/M) + e$$

Adjusted R^2 = 0.28
D. W. statistic = 1.35
SEE = 8.55
n = 15

For the year 1989 :

$$\ln INTR = -\underset{(-0.35)}{0.679} + \underset{(4.57)}{0.785} \ln GDP + \underset{(0.066)}{0.007} \ln (M/y) - \underset{(-0.245)}{0.16} \ln (x/M) + e$$

Adjusted R_2 = 0.62
D.W. statistic = 1.16 & three
SEE = 7.88
n = 15

In both cases we see that the variables (M/Y) and X/M, that is, average propensity to import and the ratio of exports to imports are not important in the explanation of the variation of international reserve. This is because their coefficient are not statistically significant.

But in both cases the coefficient of GDP is significant and while in 1984, the elasticity of GDP is 0.455, its value has increased in 1989 and it is as high as 0.785. Further, the value of adjusted R^2 has significantly increased in 1989 over 1984, that is 0.62 from 0.28.

The nature of the results show that we are to do much more indepth analysis to capture the mechanism behind the movement of international reserve of the member countries.

International Reserve And Imports One important objective of maintaining international reserve is to guard against the eventuality of blocking the inflow of funds from exports and thus meeting the demand for imports. In reality how the different countries behave is interesting to see. With that objective in view we have taken 28 countries of which 10 are developed countries and nine are developing countries. The data relate to two years, 1984 and 1989. No specific pattern is decernible among the countries depending on their level of development. While the ratio of reserve to annual imports in 1984 is 0.29 for Germany, 0.57 for Switzerland, and 0.10 for United Kingdom, while it is 0.42 for India and 0.34 for Indonesia.

But compared to 1984, the figures in 1994 are higher in general, which is the broad common feature. (Tables 5.6 and 5.7). This pattern is very much prominent in the case of the developing countries. It seems that the developing countries have become much more cautious regarding the maintenance of international reserve. Perhaps the thrust for export-led growth and the concern for the stability of the exchange rates of the currencies have induced the developing countries to maintain a good international reserve.

Table 5.6 : International Reserve And Imports Of Selected Countries: 1984

(Unit: U.S. dollar million)

	INTR	Imports	Ratio
Developed Countries			
U.S.A.	23840.0	334428.04	0.071285
Canada	2491.0	76947.18	0.032372
U.K.	9440.0	91022.33	0.103710
Japan	26429.0	128713.65	0.205331
France	20940.0	94257.71	0.222156
Sweden	3845.0	24262.53	0.158474
Switzerland	15296.0	26750.48	0.571802
Germany	40141.0	137932.02	0.291020
Italy	20796.0	76542.18	0.271693
Belgium	4564.0	50610.34	0.090179
Middle Level Countries			
Singapore	10416.0	28068.87	0.371087
Brazil	11508.0	15210.00	0.756607
Argentina	1243.0	4584.70	0.271119
Greece	954.2	8436.64	0.113101
Portugal	516.0	6700.50	0.077009
Mexico	7272.0	9919.77	0.733081
Turkey	1271.0	10735.10	0.118396
South Africa	242.0	11855.42	0.020412
Korea	2753.6	29838.05	0.092284
Developing Countries			
India	5842.0	13878.32	0.420944
Egypt	736.0	10766.07	0.068362
Pakistan	1035.0	5341.02	0.193783
Indonesia	4773.0	13882.00	0.343826
Nigeria	1462.0	8880.62	0.164628
Thailand	1921.0	9029.65	0.212743
Uruguay	34.0	768.50	0.174365
Morocco	49.0	3601.3275	0.013606
Sri Lanka	510.0	1809.0182	0.281920

Table 5.7: International Reserve And Imports Of Selected Countries: 1994

(Unit: U.S. dollar million)

	Intr	Imports	Ratio
Developed Countries			
U.S.A.	90597.98	986756.27	0.091813
Canada	12286.00	150978.04	0.081376
U.K.	64078.13	230568.75	0.277913
Japan	125860.00	281241.22	0.447516
France	26257.00	237124.95	0.110730
Sweden	23254.00	4438.52	5.239136
Switzerland	34729.00	66548.99	0.521856
Germany	77363.00	398598.91	0.194087
Italy	32265.00	165842.17	0.194552
Middle Level Countries			
Singapore	58177.00	107069.89	0.543355
Brazil	37070.00	35997.00	1.029808
Argentina	14327.00	21527.30	0.665527
Portugal	15513.00	27739.02	0.559248
Mexico	6278.00	38715.87	0.162155
Turkey	71169.00	23270.00	3.058401
South Africa	1685.00	23435.28	0.071900
Korea	25639.30	104261.44	0.245913
Developing Countries			
India	19698.00	26796.56	0.735094
Egypt	13481.00	10203.16	1.321257
Pakistan	2929.00	8822.86	0.331978
Indonesia	12133.00	31985.00	0.379334
Thailand	29332.00	54564.53	0.537565
Uruguay	969.00	2772.60	0.349491
Morocco	4352.00	7379.35	0.589753
Sri Lanka	2046.00	4722.49	0.433246

Conclusion The demand for international reserve has the wider implication regarding the concern of the economists for the maintenance of an optimum level of international liquidity so that world trade and commerce can run smoothly. There is another implication of the maintenance of international reserve of a single country and that is that the level of international reserve can be used to stabilise the exchange rate of the country's currency apart from utilising the reserve to meet imbalance in the current account in the short run. This subject has been pursued here.

Many developing countries suffer from the apprehension of default of their import bill due to inadequate international reserve. Because such an eventuality hampers the country's credit rating and it becomes difficult for the country with poor rating to raise finance in the international capital market. For this many countries set a target of the level of international reserve equivalent to six to eight months' import bill, though there is no hard and fast rule about the exact number of months.

As indicated earlier, holding a sizable international reserve is costly for a developing country because the opportunity cost of holding it is positive. One can argue that the maintenance of a high level of international reserve is equivalent to giving subsidised credit to the rich and developed countries as it is the latter whose currencies are convertible and other countries keep in their portfolio.

An empirical exercise has been done about the ratio of international reserve and yearly import bill. There is no clear correlation between the level of economic development and the ratio of international reserve to annual imports. Perhaps a better system of payments flow in the international monetary mechanism will reduce the need of maintaining a high level of international reserve, because the liability of meeting the import bill can be matched by the inflow of foreign payments for the country's exports.

From a theoretical standpoint exports of a country depend on the purchasing power of the rest of the world, though import depend on the domestic purchasing power. Sometimes, an asymmetry in the rates of growth of national income at home and abroad can create a gap in the balance of trade (current account) and this is to be bridged by the change in the international reserve or by capital movement. In either case a decent level of international reserve can give the country both a breathing space and a respectability regarding the financing of a negative current account gap.

Further, one should consider the size of foreign debt of a country along with the size of international reserve. A higher volume of foreign debt necessitates higher liability of redemption of the debt along with the volatility of the amount of payments due to exchange rate fluctuations. In this situation same level of comforts can be preserved only by a higher level of international reserve.

The situation of a country like India with huge volume of import of gold per year is unique in the sense that this accumulation of gold, though more or less transparent, is not part of official reserve. Thus every year a large volume of foreign exchange earned by the country is being converted into gold and the latter is entering into the economy through illegal routes. This augments the size of the investment portfolio of private individuals but the society is badly affected at least on two counts. First, the country is losing foreign exchange by this import. Second, this gold is largely created as durable consumption good. But people use this gold partly as a hedge against future potential price rise and partly to dodge government taxes. A more transparency of the market system and stability of the price level can reduce the largely unproductive consumption of gold. Then the size of the international reserve can reflect the savings of the economy.

One implication of the above argument is that India should introduce more transparent policy regarding the purchase and holding of gold by the individuals. Gold should be brought in the mainstream of financial transactions through the banking system, may be, by the introduction of gold banking, as practised in some countries. This will increase institutional savings on the one hand, and reduce the demand for foreign exchange for the purchase of gold on the other.

Recently many developing countries have opted for the current account convertibility of their currencies. This along with the increasing volatility in the foreign exchange market in the world have created additional responsibility to the monetary authority to maintain adequate liquidity in foreign exchange to deal with the situation of an attack on the domestic currency. The strength of the Hong Kong dollar is widely known because of the pegging of the currency to U.S. dollar and the currency board system. The latter ensures that for every Hong Kong dollar issued to the system, U.S. dollar is added to the reserve at the fixed rate U.S.D.1 = H.K.D.$7.8 . Even in this case HK dollar comes under attack in the currency market. The countries which are not fortunate enough like Hong Kong regarding the huge volume of international reserve often find themselves at the receiving end whenever their currencies comes under attack in the foreign exchange market. Considering the fact that maintenance of the international reserve involves some cost, the stability question of the domestic currency compels the developing countries to maintain additional international reserve and at a cost. This is a new dimension in today's world of flexible exchange rate system. The guardian of the world financial order, the International Monetary Fund, though considered to be the lender of the last resort, is a mere spectator in this situation. Because of this and also for the financial crisis emerging in Latin America and Russia for which IMF has no financial strength to cope with, there has been a serious discussion going on for a more fundamental change in the world financial order. It seems logical that the world financial institutions should think afresh for the solution to this type of instability as described in this paragraph.

References :

1. Archibald G. C. and J. Richmond, On the Theory of Foreign Exchange Requirement, Review of Economic Studies, April 1971, 38(2), 245-63.

2. Baumol, W.J., The Transaction Demand for Cash, Quarterly Journal of Economics, November, 1952, 66, 545-56.

3. Ben-Bassat A. and D. Gottliab, Optimal Institutional Reserves and Sovereign Risk, Journal of Institutional Economics, 33, 1992, 345-362.

4. Brown, W.M., The External Liquidity of an Advanced Country, Princeton Studies in International Finance, No. 14, Princeton, Princeton University Press, 1964.

5. Caves, R.E., International Liquidity: Toward a Home Repair Manual, Review of Economics and Statistics, May 1964, 46, 173-80.

6. Clark, P.B., Optimum International Reserve and the Speed of Adjustment, Journal of Political Economy, March-April, 1970, 78, 356-76.

7. __________, Demand for International Reserve: A Cross Country Analysis, Canadian Journal of Economics, 3 (1), February 1970, 577-94.

8. Clark, P.B., Interest Payments and the Rate of Return on International Fiat Currency, Duke University, Memio, 1971.

9. Clower R and R Lipsey, The Present State of International Liquidity Theory, American Economic Review, May 1968, 58(2).

10. Cooper R N, The Relevance and International Liquidity to Developed Countries, American Economic Review, May 1968.

11.Courchene T.J. and G. M. Yoursef, The Demand for International Reserve, Journal of Political Economy, August, 1967, 75(4), 404-13.

12. Edwards S. The Role of International Reserve and Foreign Debt in the External Adjustment Process, in Joaquin Muns (ed.), Adjustment, Conditionality and International Financing, IMF, Washington DC., 1984.

13.__________, On the Interest Rate Elasticity of the Demand for International Reserve : Some Evidence from Developing Countries, Journal of International Money and Finance, 4, 1985, 287-95.

14. Edwards, S, The Demand for International Reserves and Monetary Equilibrium : Some Evidence from Developing Countries, Review of Economics and Statistics, 66, 1984, 495-500.

15. Flanders M.J., International Liquidity is always Inadequate, Kyklos, 1969, 22(3), 519-29.

16.__________, The Demand for International Reserves, Princeton Studies in International Finance, No. 27, 1971, Princeton University Press.

17. Fleming, J.M., Towards Assessing the need for International Reserves, Essays in International Finance, No. 58, Princeton University. Press, 1967.

18. Fond J.L. and G. Huang, The Demand for International Reserve in China : An ECM Model with Domestic Monetary Equilibrium, Economica, 1994, 67, 379-97.

19. Frenkel, J. A., The Demand for International Reserves by Developed and Less-Developed Countries, Economica, February, 1974, 14-24.

20.______________, International Reserves : Pegged Exchange Rates and Managed Float, in K. Brunner and A. H. Metzler (eds.) Economic Policies in Open Economies, Carnegie-Rochester Conference Series on Public Policy, Vol. 9, Amsterdam, North-Holland.

21.____________, International Liquidity and Monetary Control, in G. M. von Furstenbug (ed.), International Money and Credit : The Policy Roles, Washington DC, IMF, 1983.

22. Frenkel J. A. and B. Javanovic, Optimal International Reserve: a Stochastic Framework, Economic Journal, 91, 1981, 507-14.

23. Friedman, M., The Optimum Quantity of Money, Chicago, Aldine Publishing Company, 1969.

24. Gilbert, M., Problems of the International Monetary System, Essays in International Finance, Princeton University Press, 1966.

25.______________, The Gold-Dollar System : Conditions of Equilibrium and the Price of Gold, Essays in International Finance, Princeton University Press, 1968.

26. Gottlieb, D., On the Determinants of a Country's Credit worthiness : The case of the Israel 1971-1983, Journal of Economic Development, 14, 1989 65-91.

27. Grubel, H.G., Gold and the Dollar Crisis Five Years Later, Nat. Bank Review, September 1965, 3 (1), 89-99.

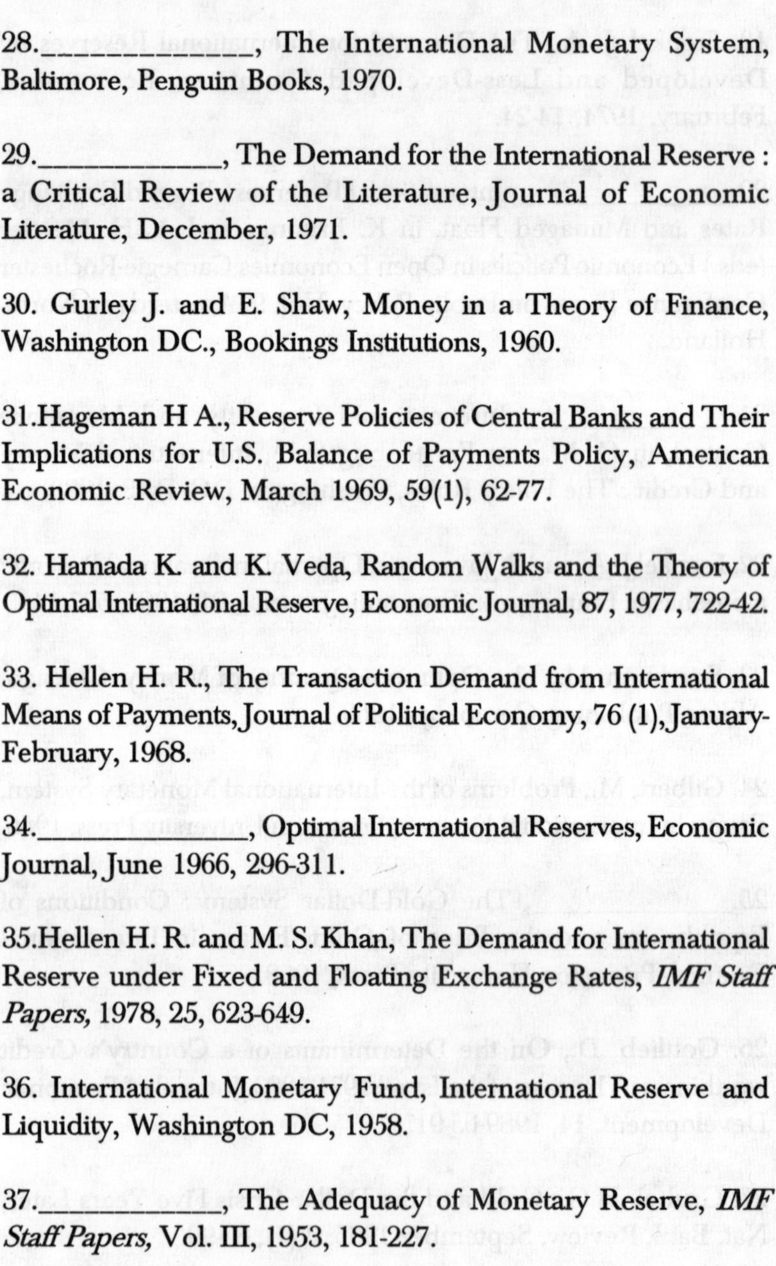

28.______________, The International Monetary System, Baltimore, Penguin Books, 1970.

29.______________, The Demand for the International Reserve : a Critical Review of the Literature, Journal of Economic Literature, December, 1971.

30. Gurley J. and E. Shaw, Money in a Theory of Finance, Washington DC., Bookings Institutions, 1960.

31.Hageman H A., Reserve Policies of Central Banks and Their Implications for U.S. Balance of Payments Policy, American Economic Review, March 1969, 59(1), 62-77.

32. Hamada K. and K. Veda, Random Walks and the Theory of Optimal International Reserve, Economic Journal, 87, 1977, 722-42.

33. Hellen H. R., The Transaction Demand from International Means of Payments, Journal of Political Economy, 76 (1), January-February, 1968.

34.______________, Optimal International Reserves, Economic Journal, June 1966, 296-311.

35.Hellen H. R. and M. S. Khan, The Demand for International Reserve under Fixed and Floating Exchange Rates, *IMF Staff Papers,* 1978, 25, 623-649.

36. International Monetary Fund, International Reserve and Liquidity, Washington DC, 1958.

37.______________, The Adequacy of Monetary Reserve, *IMF Staff Papers,* Vol. III, 1953, 181-227.

38.____________, International Reserves : Needs and Availability, Washington DC, IMF, 1970.

39. Jyosha, M. A., The Optimal Balance of Payments Strategy of a Less Developed Country, Discussion Paper 161, February 1971, Department of Economics, SUNY, Buffalo, 1971.

40. Johnson, H. G., The International Competitive Position of the United States and the Balance of Payments Prospects for 1968, Review of Economics and Statistics, February, 1964.

41.____________, International Trade and Economic Growth, Cambridge, Mass., Havard University Press, 1958.

42. Kane, E J., International Liquidity : a Probabilistic Approach, Kyklos, 18(1), 1965, 27-48.

43. Kelly M. G., The Demand for Intenational Reserves, American Economic Review, September 1970, 55(A), 655-67.

44. Kennen P., Reserve Asset Preferences of Central Banks and Stability of the Gold Exchange Standard, Princeton Studies in International Finance University Press 1963.

45. Kenin P. and E. Yudin, The Demand for Intenational Reserves, Review of Economics and Statistics, August 1965, 47 242-50.

46.____________, Demand for International Reserves : A Reply, Review of Economics and Stat., 1967, 49, 626-27.

47. Kindleberger C. P., Balance of Payments Deficits and the International Reserves, Review of Economics and Statistics, August 1965, 47, 242-50.

48.___________, Demand for International Reserves : A Reply, Review of Economics and Stat., 1967, 49, 626-27.

49. Kindleberger C P, Balance of Payments Deficits and the International Markets for Liquidity, Princeton Essays in International Finance, No. 46, 1965.

50. Krause, L.B., A Passive Balance of Payments Strategy for the United States, Bookings Papers on Economic Activity, 1970.

51. Landell-Mills, J.M., The Demand for International Reserves and their Opportunity Costs, *IMF Staff Papers,* 36, 1989, 708-31.

52. Lapittus, J.R., The Demand for Official Reserves to Finance International Trade under a system of Fixed Exchange Rates, Unpublished Ph.D. dissertation, Yale University 1970.

53. Lizando J.S. and D.J. Mathieson, The Stability of the Demand for International Reserve, Journal of International Money and Finance, 1987, 6, 251-82.

54. Machlup, F., From Dormant Liabilities to Dormant Assets, The Banker, 117, 1967, 788-97.

55.___________, The Need for Monetary Reserves, Banca Naz. Lavaro Quarterly Review, September, 1966, 78, 175-225.

56. Makin J., The Compositions of International Reserve Holding: The Problems of Choice Involving Risk, American Economic Review, December 1971.

57. Markovitz, H., Portfolio Selection : Efficient Diversification of Investments, New York, Wiley, 1959.

58. Mckinnon, R.I., Private and Official International Money : The Case for the Dollar, Princeton Essays in International Finance No. 74, Princeton, University 1969.

59. Moore, B.J., An Introduction to the Theory of Finance, New York, Free Press, 1968.

60. Mundell R.A., International Economics, Macmillan, London, 1968.

61.________, Monetary Theory : Inflation, Interest and Growth in the World Economy, Goodyear, Pacific Palisades, 1971.

62. Olivera, H.G., A Note on the Optical Rate of Growth of International Reserve, Journal of Political Economy, March-April, 1969, 77(2), 245-48.

63. Salant W. A., The Reserve Currency Role of the Dollar : Blessing or Burden on the U.S.? Review of Economics and Statistics, May 1964.

64. Samuelson, P.A., What Classical and Neoclassical Monetary Theory Really Was, Canadian Journal of Economics, 1968, 1(1) 1-15.

65. Scitovsky T., Economic Theory and Western European Integration, Stanford, Stanford University Press, 1958.

66. Stekler L. and R. Piekarz, Reserve Asset Compositions for Major Central Banks Oxford Economic Papers, July 1970 22(2), 260-74.

67. Thorn R., The Demand for International Reserve : A Note on Behalf of the Rejected Hypothesis, Review of Economics and Statistics, November, 1967, 49, 623-27.

68. Tobin J., The Interest-Elasticity of Transaction Demand for Cash, Review of Economics and Statistics, August, 1956, 38, 241-47.

69.__________, Liquidity Preference as Behaviour Towards Risks, Review of Economic Studies, February 1958, 25, 65-86.

70.Triffin, R.., Gold and the Dollar Crisis, New Haven, Yale University Press, 1960.

71. Willett,T., Adequacy of International Means of Payments, Review of Economics and Statistics, August 1969, 51(3), 373-74.

72. Williamson,J., International Liquidity : A Survey, Economic Journal, September 1973.

73. Yeager, L.B., The Misconceived Problem of International Liquidity, Journal of Finance, September 1959, 24, 347-60.

Appendix 1.

Observation	*Country's Name*
OBS1	India
OBS2	Japan
OBS3	Australia
OBS4	New Zealand
OBS5	Indonesia
OBS6	Malaysia
OBS7	Thailand
OBS8	Turkey
OBS9	Egypt
OBS10	Algeria
OBS11	Sri Lanka
OBS12	Hungary
OBS13	Denmark
OBS14	Belgium
OBS15	Iran
OBS16	Brazil
OBS17	Argentina
OBS18	Chile
OBS19	Uruguay
OBS20	Nigeria
OBS21	Ghana
OBS22	Sweden
OBS23	United Kingdom
OBS24	U.S.A.
OBS25	Canada
OBS26	Mexico
OBS27	South Aferica
OBS28	Italy
OBS29	Spain
OBS30	France
OBS31	Austrla
OBS32	Portugal
OBS33	Phili ppines
OBS34	Korea

Appendix 2

Table 5A2.1 : Economic indicators of 34 countries 1984

(U.S. dollar in million)

OBS	Mon	Price	GDP	EXR	INTR	Gold	Imports	Exports
1	29182.3290	134.60	172186.9700	12.4510	5842.00	184.00	13878.3230	8630.9533
2	343986.4500	100.70	1186571.0000	251.1000	26429.00	831.00	128713.6500	160593.3800
3	14722.4230	134.70	163291.8200	0.8278	7441.00	2539.00	24469.7680	21867.9920
4	1796.1580	152.00	18467.3590	0.4776	1787.00	1.00	5224.4664	4577.3661
5	7990.6890	158.40	79994.4130	1074.0000	4773.00	947.00	20.3929	12.9255
6	5508.0412	125.10	31546.3910	2.4250	3723.00	80.00	13577.7310	15936.9070
7	2861.8784	110.80	36528.5450	27.1500	1921.00	768.00	9029.6500	6454.4014
8	1849.8448	340.20	422.7796	444.7400	1271.00	800.00	9073.5327	5864.6278
9	17776.0690	150.70	43364.4380	1.4286	736.00	679.00	10765.8570	3139.8571
10	35222.2460	140.10	50734.9630	5.1227	1464.00	192.00	10005.2700	12446.6130
11	633.4475	193.73	5807.2678	26.2800	510.00	11.00	1809.0182	1421.1187
12	4158.6749	122.40	19109.7480	51.1990	2109.00	466.00	7627.1020	8086.0954
13	13662.5220	144.00	50252.2200	11.2600	3008.90	545.00	15259.9460	14683.3920
14	14790.7410	131.70	71544.0710	63.0800	4564.00	1443.00	50662.6500	47.4337
16	7251.8844	3606.00	12153.8940	3184.0000	11508.00	488.00	15210.0000	27005.0000
17	2524.3370	23175.00	2954.2296	0.1787	1243.00	192.00	4584.7000	8107.4000

18	906.1135	211.50	14764.5040	128.2400	2302.90	540.10	3574.0000	3657.0000
19	298.3165	428.85	3980.4175	74.2500	134.00	647.00	776.7000	933.8000
20	15098.7880	223.80	70169.0350	1.2372	1462.00	24.00	8883.6633	11247.5240
21	536.9800	844.30	5411.2200	0.0200	301.60	11.50	437.7400	387.9200
22	10643.5280	150.00	87563.2680	8.9895	3845.00	208.00	24313.9210	27010.2890
23	60357.7350	132.10	369328.2700	1.1565	9.44	5.48	91325.3350	81519.3720
24	584665.7000	115.40	3709716.1000	1.0250	23.84	11.10	355019.0000	229579.5000
25	38981.3830	125.80	330013.6200	1.3214	2.49	691.00	76241.8640	88515.9670
26	12181.1380	686.00	2279.2895	192.5600	7272.00	709.00	10070.0000	20410.0000
27	11795.4690	154.90	52780.6070	0.5038	242.00	2039.00	11855.4210	12773.8490
28	177632000.0000	160.80	316189.8800	1935.9000	20796.00	21637.00	77209.0500	67584.0690
29	33039.2150	166.30	149567.4700	173.4000	11955.00	3832.00	26695.5010	21788.3500
30	110195.9900	155.10	446517.9300	9.5920	20940.00	26832.00	94829.0240	88714.5530
31	8000.0000	116.40	12918.3670	22.0500	4244.00	1793.00	17781.8590	14263.0380
32	47.3169	230.20	16573.1330	169.2800	516.00	5174.00	6856.0964	4493.1474
33	1701.9230	246.10	2775.6578	19.7600	602.00	288.00	5448.8866	4470.5971
34	8243.8965	127.20	8112.8837	827.4000	2753.60	31.10	2983.0460	28488.0340

Mon - Money Supply
GDP - Gross Domestic Product
EXR - Exchange Rate
INTR - International Reserve

Table 5A2.2: Economic indicators of 34 countries, 1989

OBS	MON	Price	GDP	EXR	INTR	Gold	Imports	Exports
1	7979.7838	98.00	2761917.000	143.450	83957.00	161.00	19656.589	15129.204
2	43845.0240	91.70	268212.500	17.035	3859.00	1114.00	202028.580	263666.780
3	34493.5470	94.40	283310.980	0.793	13780.00	3248.00	45026.152	37766.606
4	12769.3300	95.60	42646.052	0.597	3027.00	1.00	8784.812	8850.205
5	11440.7340	90.90	93035.614	1797.000	5454.00	1044.00	12.332	9.151
6	8130.0632	99.10	37948.803	2.703	7783.00	109.00	22512.484	25089.335
7	6800.3114	96.70	72284.935	25.690	9515.00	993.00	25795.212	20097.898
8	8251.7180	65.70	95151.056	2313.700	4780.00	1354.00	14592.211	10726.974
9	20428.1810	85.60	69818.181	1.100	1520.00	679.00	15112.454	5213.364
10	31126.7430	110.10	39840.637	8.032	847.00	257.00	8724.104	8956.300
11	877.2000	81.90	6297.275	40.000	244.00	10.00	1980.625	1404.375
12	5676.0948	82.00	27353.980	62.543	1246.00	479.00	8293.494	9134.515
13	34217.6150	99.00	115685.530	6.608	6397.00	711.00	29527.391	31068.401
14	33763.9820	101.00	168680.080	35.760	10766.00	1277.00	108610.170	110265.650
16	912760.2900	28280.00	968523.000	4.130	7535.00	1194.00	19875.000	34383.000
17	1520.8913	66127.00	18072.424	0.180	1463.00	1421.00	4203.200	9579.300
18	93517.7140	174.20	338832.290	4.722	17960.00	587.00	7144.000	8080.000

19	475.9066	48.20	60100.060	0.805	501.00	855.00	1173.800	1593.600
20	3485.0346	226.20	29381.388	7.651	1766.00	2.00	4033.460	7576.918
21	615.0876	81.50	4676.765	303.030	347.30	78.30	1.145	0.908
22		95.50	197944.430	6.227	9559.00	279.00	50841.496	53407.740
23	313570.2000	94.10	321370.280	1.606	34.77	5.46	195387.740	150549.340
24	1065047.6000	96.60	6730475.400	1.282	63.55	11.06	384552.970	466434.200
25	82440.8360	99.70	562057.350	1.158	16055.00	741.00	1222530.660	124588.010
26	11013.6310	81.10	192206.730	2.641	6329.00	709.00	17143.846	18154.615
27	17091.0110	89.30	94888.770	0.394	960.00	1137.00	19092.400	23029.485
28	3558.3628	93.10	9393.939	1270.500	46720.00	26496.00	16521.841	151820.540
29	123459.7100	97.90	410535.900	109.720	41467.00	5419.00	76525.701	46796.390
30	282135.4500	101.30	1064219.000	5.788	24611.00	33982.00	212465.440	197519.000
31	19889.9700	97.20	141591.190	11.815	8598.00	3277.00	43562.420	36336.013
32	12702.8830	150.80	47899.092	149.840	9952.00	5184.00	20042.712	13452.490
33	3622.1033	90.80	41238.859	22.440	1417.00	959.00	10829.456	7527.986
34	21082.9890	96.00	219489.400	679.600	15213.60	31.60	60728.369	61628.899

Table 5A2.3 : International reserve of countries : 1994

Country	SDR	FEX	Gold	Resp	TR-Gold
India	2.00	19386.000	3355.00	310.00	19698.00
Korea	76.30	25032.100	33.60	530.80	25639.30
Japan	2083.00	115146.000	1238.00	8631.00	125860.00
Thailand	32.00	28884.000	947.00	416.00	29332.00
Turkey	1.00	7121.000	1410.00	47.00	7169.00
France	362.00	23520.000	30730.00	2375.00	26257.00
Spain	255.00	40205.000	4217.00	1109.00	41569.00
Portugal	71.00	15106.000	5185.00	337.00	15513.00
Germany	1114.00	72219.000	8839.00	4030.00	77363.00
Turkey	1.00	7121.000	1410.00	47.00	7169.00
Greece	3.00	14321.600	850.90	166.00	14487.90
Italy	125.00	30107.000	26342.00	2033.00	32265.00
U.S.A.	10.04	60177.078	16131.90	812.00	92382.47
Canada	1148.00	10219.000	198.00	17562.60	12286.00
Argentina	563.00	13764.000	1651.00	919.00	14327.00
Australia	73.00	10706.000	3023.00	506.00	11285.00
Egypt	86.00	13316.000	694.00	78.00	13481.00

Poland	1.50	5727.700	189.00	112.60	5841.80
Hungary	2.00	6727.000	42.00	82.00	6810.00
Sweden	68.00	22527.000	310.00	659.00	23254.00
Malaysia	135.00	24888.000	122.00	400.00	25423.00
United Kingdom	0.49	60203.125	8296.88	3109.38	64078.13
Ghana	4.20	554.300	77.20	25.40	583.90
Denmark	182.00	8444.000	703.00	430.00	9056.00
China	539.00	51620.000	646.00	755.00	52914.00
Phili ppines	24.00	5866.000	1104.00	127.00	6017.00
Bahrain	16.10	1092.000	6.60	61.60	1169.70
Norway	389.40	17992.400	42.10	643.70	19025.50
Nepal	0.10	685.100	6.50	8.40	693.60
Bangladesh	36.00	3102.600	27.20	0.10	3138.70

SDR – special drawing rights
FEX – foreign exchange reserve
RESP – short term foreign exchange holding in convertible currencies
TR-Gold – International reserve minus gold
Unit – U.S.$

Appendix 3

(*Unit : U.S. dollar million*)

Table 5A3.1
INDIA

Year	Mon	Price	GDP	EXR	IN TR	Gold
1970	9049.1	166.0	53975.2	7.5	1006	243
1971	10590.7	172.3	59417.5	7.3	1206	264
1972	10649.4	186.0	60015.0	8.0	1180	264
1973	12445.3	133.5	72799.5	8.1	1142	293
1974	13773.2	170.0	86697.2	8.1	1325	298
1975	13688.0	172.5	81630.3	8.9	1373	284
1976	17201.9	98.1	86918.1	8.9	2792	205
1977	21744.4	105.3	106127.4	8.2	4872	235
1978	24542.0	105.2	117660.0	8.2	6426	262
1979	29559.9	119.2	135879.6	7.9	7432	284
1980	25959.6	141.1	171261.0	7.9	6944	284
1981	25583.0	158.1	163402.6	9.1	4693	248
1982	28410.8	115.0	184336.7	9.6	4315	234
1983	28541.9	124.0	197531.7	10.5	4937	215

1984	28594.5	134.6	155859.0	12.5	5842	184
1985	33147.3	142.4	215288.5	12.2	6420	203
1986	35618.0	150.1	223129.1	13.1	6396	209
1987	41318.6	159.1	256628.1	12.9	6454	213
1988	39994.0	121.3	261663.0	14.9	4899	183
1989	42952.7	131.1	259917.8	17.0	3859	161
1990	46279.0	143.1	293736.5	18.1	1521	3667
1991	40226.1	162.9	235929.4	25.8	3627	3168
1992	44843.5	181.4	269301.5	26.2	5757	2908
1993	41822.8	136.4	250592.7	31.4	10199	3325
1994	52683.2	150.8	280337.8	31.4	19698	3355

Note : Abbreviations as explainesd in earlier tables.

Table 5A3.2
PORTUGAL

(U.S. dollar million)

Year	GDP	EXR	INTR	Imports	Exports
1970	6267.826	28.75	602.00	1554.782	946.087
1971	7825.835	27.56	945.00	1846.879	1077.649
1972	8703.704	27.00	1291.00	2207.407	1300.000
1973	10916.827	25.85	1676.00	2831.721	1733.075
1974	13792.682	24.60	1161.00	4605.691	2337.398
1975	13731.343	27.47	398.00	3549.326	1794.685
1976	14862.123	31.55	176.00	4050.713	1733.756
1977	15699.949	39.86	366.00	4583.542	1899.147
1978	17111.497	46.01	871.00	5001.086	2314.714
1979	19997.991	49.78	931.00	6430.293	3425.070
1980	23680.241	53.04	795.00	8782.051	4377.828
1981	23005.363	65.25	534.00	9190.804	3906.513
1982	20777.004	89.06	447.00	8466.202	3724.455
1983	17510.079	131.45	385.00	6842.145	3869.152
1984	16633.388	169.28	516.00	6856.096	4493.147

1985	22375.388	157.49	1395.00	8272.271	6142.612
1986	30251.847	146.12	1456.00	9872.022	7406.926
1987	39845.229	129.87	3327.00	15132.82	10094.710
1988	41011.000	146.37	5127.00	17633.39	10808.225
1989	47899.092	149.84	9952.00	20181.52	13452.349
1990	64076.347	133.60	14485.00	26968.56	17483.532
1991	74046.057	134.18	20629.00	28402.14	17532.419
1992	77289.452	146.76	19129.00	27889.07	16856.772
1993	–	176.81	15840.00	21995.36	13992.421
1994	–	159.09	15513.00	27682.44	18228.675

Note: Abbreviations as explainesd in earlier tables.

Table 5A3.3
SPAIN

(U.S. dollar in million)

Year	GDP	EXR	INTR	Imports	Exports
1970	37722.317	69.72	1319	4766.207	2398.164
1971	44956.073	66.02	2727	5269.615	3115.722
1972	54789.995	63.57	4473	6902.627	3858.738
1973	73731.343	56.95	6170	9861.282	5311.677
1974	91659.240	56.11	5874	15843.878	7282.124
1975	101037.300	59.77	5506	15596.453	7386.649
1976	106413.820	68.29	4704	17138.673	8544.443
1977	113953.770	80.91	5977	16692.621	9582.252
1978	160961.340	70.11	10112	20417.914	14283.269
1979	199561.600	66.15	13224	25761.148	18461.073
1980	191394.320	79.25	11863	30923.659	18841.640
1981	174910.210	97.45	10805	30481.272	19378.142
1982	157030.250	125.60	7655	27592.356	17977.707
1983	143790.680	156.70	7402	26652.839	18114.869
1984	147174.160	173.40	11955	26695.501	21788.350

1985	182945.180	154.15	11175	32910.801	26592.280
1986	244138.970	132.40	14755	36939.577	28714.501
1987	331596.330	109.00	30669	55320.183	38491.743
1988	353979.720	113.45	37074	62049.360	41308.065
1989	410535.900	109.72	41467	77031.192	46796.390
1990	517438.860	96.91	51228	91989.474	58227.221
1991	567804.320	96.69	65822	100032.060	64388.251
1992	514761.820	114.62	45504	89033.327	57631.303
1993	428268.050	142.21	41045	73148.161	56130.370
1994	490913.920	131.74	41569	93730.074	74352.512

Table 5A3.4
JAPAN

(U.S . dollar million)

Year	GDP	EXR	INTR	Imports	Exports
1970	205074.79	357.65	4308	19004.613	19443.590
1971	256356.41	314.80	14622	21950.444	26661.372
1972	305940.39	302.00	17564	23937.086	29158.940
1973	401778.57	280.00	11355	37157.142	35825.000
1974	446067.45	300.95	12614	60033.228	53895.996
1975	486078.97	305.15	11950	56287.071	5437.717
1976	568896.85	292.80	15746	65672.814	68066.939
1977	773425.00	240.00	22341	79716.666	90200.000
1978	1050380.20	194.60	32407	85960.945	105477.900
1979	924267.83	239.70	19522	101147.26	94000.834
1980	1183133.00	203.00	24636	157610.83	144738.910
1981	1173092.30	219.90	28208	143083.21	152201.000
1982	1151493.60	235.00	23334	138961.7	146523.400
1983	1213466.80	232.20	24602	129263.56	150344.530
1984	1196905.60	251.10	26429	128713.65	160593.380

1985	1598099.70	200.50	26719	154992.51	209271.820
1986	2103136.30	159.10	42257	135455.68	221816.460
1987	2821255.00	123.50	80973	176024.29	269765.180
1988	2951362.70	125.85	96728	190758.83	269590.780
1989	2761917.00	143.45	83957	202028.58	263666.780
1990	3158757.40	134.40	78501	251889.88	308459.820
1991	3604608.60	125.20	72059	254792.33	338330.670
1992	3712585.10	124.75	71623	236689.37	344777.550
1993	4166043.80	111.85	98524	239821.18	359409.920
1994	4704632.00	99.74	125860	281241.22	405754.960

Table 5A3.5
UNITED KINGDOM

(U.S. dollar million)

Year	MON	Price	GDP	EXR	INTR	Gold	Imports	Exports
70	4027.24	28.02	123921.84	2.3937	1480	1350	21813.79	19379.35
71	4344.76	30.55	147406.87	2.5525	7990	840	25011.94	23151.18
72	5391.59	32.17	151828.14	2.3481	4850	800	26000.51	22546.46
73	5724.86	34.52	172520.83	2.3232	5590	890	36527.67	28080.52
74	6276.35	42.60	196945.21	2.3485	6040	890	54341.94	38301.69
75	8638.49	52.43	214187.47	2.0235	4600	890	48657.08	39674.76
76	11436.79	60.91	213225.60	1.7024	3370	890	52917.40	43031.56
77	12339.98	72.00	278237.88	1.9060	20110	940	69033.41	60971.94
78	13448.02	79.11	342874.28	2.0345	16030	960	80429.89	71980.61
79	13426.26	87.69	440841.28	2.2240	19740	3260	104361.20	90376.69
80	13014.68	100.00	552771.45	2.3850	20650	6990	118708.60	112946.44
81	19145.70	109.55	486406.44	1.9080	15240	7330	97630.45	97304.18
82	25184.27	118.02	450510.08	1.6145	12400	4560	91990.98	89698.39
83	31152.63	124.41	441649.67	1.4506	11340	5910	95886.11	88028.21
84	45101.59	132.08	376845.52	1.1565	9440	5480	91325.34	81519.37

85	42658.36	139.42	516177.63	1.4445	12860	4310	122821.50	113237.24
86	51007.12	145.72	567446.58	1.4745	18420	4900	127066.51	107620.80
87	82351.06	86.70	792355.67	1.8715	41720	5790	175969.65	149437.40
88	94318.87	89.80	853052.58	1.8095	44100	6470	192840.22	147754.72
89	121650.6	94.10	828373.78	1.6055	34770	5460	195387.74	150549.34
90	111483.4	100.00	1062559.30	1.9280	35850	5240	243093.80	199918.17
91	122531.7	105.40	1076251.10	1.8707	41890	5040	222212.97	196193.40
92	157890.2	108.70	903026.88	1.5120	36640	4770	190310.90	164064.09
93	170240.3	113.00	888115.36	1.4812	36780	4560	203522.80	179130.40
94	170764.8	115.80	1045109.30	1.5625	41010	5310	230494.96	207792.86

APPENDIX A

EUROPEAN UNION AND EURO

A NEW CURRENCY EURO EMERGED on January 1, 1999 which has been the currency of European Union consisting at present 11 countries. Till January 1, 2002 Euro will be the currency of the accounting system in banks, financial institutions and in the transaction of the European Union with the outside world. After that date Euro will come into circulation with the national currencies in the member countries. During the period from January 1, 2002 and June 30, 2002, every member country will have a dual currency system. During this phase, legal currencies will be progressively withdrawn and these will be replaced by Euro. After July 1, 2002, Euro will be the sole legal tender in the member countries of European Union. This is a unique experiment and its history and other implications are described in the following paragraphs.

There has been realignment in the political boundaries in the world many a time and currencies have been born or have disappeared with the changes. The closing years of the present century are the witness of both these phenomena. While some new currencies are born with the disintegration of former

U.S.S.R., some elite currencies of Europe will disappear with the full integration of European Union. As stated in the beginnng the new currency Euro of the European Union has emerged after a long negotiation. The new currency Euro will be the logical transformation of the initial European Currency Unit (ECU) which came into being in December 1978 with the establishment of European Monetary System. The European Council, at its meeting on December 5, 1978 took the resolution in which the following lines were stated : (i) a European Currency Unit (ECU) will be at the centre of the European Monetary System and ECU will be used as the denominator for the exchange rate mechanism and for operations for both the intervention and the credit mechanism; (ii) the ECU will be used as a means of settlement between monetary authorities of the European Communities; (iii) the weights of the currency in the ECU will be reexamined and if necessary revised within six months of the entry into force of the system (which began on March 13, 1979) and thereafter every five years, or on request if the weight of a particular currency of the Union has changed by 25 per cent or more.

The European Currency basket was introduced first in 1974 and it was renamed as European Currency Unit with no change being made to its composition as a basket of a fixed proportion of the currencies of each of the member states. Until the signing of the Maastricht Treaty, the currencies of all the members were included in the basket and it was revised at the interval of five years. Greek drachma was incorporated in 1984 and Spanish peseta and Portuguese escudo were included in 1989. The intention originally was that the weight of each currency in the basket should reflect the relative economy's importance of the respective countries. The option for periodic adjustment was there. However, under the Maastricht Treaty the option for revisions at five-year intervals has been abolished. The result has been that the currencies of the newly admitted members like Austria, Finland and Sweden will never be included in the currency basket. At present the weights of the currencies in ECU have seized to reflect the relevant importance of the economies and it is intended to follow the performance of the strongest currencies.

The constitution of ECU can be explained with the help of Table 1.

Table1: ECU and its composition

Country	Portion of national currencies in basket	U.S. dollar equivalent	Relative weight(%)
Deutschmark	0.6242	0.43	33.34
French franc	1.332	0.27	20.49
British pound	0.08784	0.14	10.44
Italian lira	151.8	0.09	7.17
Dutch guilder	0.2198	0.14	10.47
Belgian franc	3.301	0.11	8.57
Spanish peseta	6.885	0.06	4.24
Danish krone	0.1976	0.04	2.72
Irish punat	0.00855	0.014	1.04
Portuguese escudo	1.393	0.009	0.71
Greek drachma	1.44	0.006	0.47
Luxembourg franc	0.13	0.004	0.34
ECU	Theoretical value 1.3	100	

The ECU first emerged in the area of private transactions as book money. On the one hand all the conventional currencies are being used as means of payments in coin or note form, the ECU started out as non-physical money, that is money that was transferred from one account to another by means of electronic transfers, payment orders, credit cards or cheques. In the private market of ECU individuals used the official definitions regarding the ECU interest rates and exchange rates. Since ECU can be related to its component currencies through the fixed relationship of the composition, a clear relationship exists between the actual ECU interest rates and the exchange rates and their theoretical balance. Like any other traded asset ECU is subject to the laws of demand and supply and ECU becomes more expensive in reality compared with the theoretical value if demand exceeds supply and in that case the rate of interest declines. Such imbalances in the ECU money market are handled by the "basket makers," the latter trade ECUs against basket currencies. The differentials between the theoretical and the actual ECU exchange rates and money market rates are generally very small and these reflect the low emergence of the basket makers. But the differential is generally higher on the bond market, because arbitrageurs' operations are difficult to accomplish. When the Maastricht Treaty was ratified, the actual received appreciated sharply compared to its theoretical value, but the actual ECU rate of interest declined in a comparative manner.

Observers who have been studying the ECU market for some time are of the opinion that uncertainty will be associated with the future value of ECU as the currency approaches its transformation into the Euro when its exchange rate and interest rate will no longer be affected by the component currency. The ECU will cease to exist as a basket currency with the start of Euro, but the ECU market will continue right upto that date. The Maastricht Treaty states that the ECU will remain unchanged in value at the split second that it becomes the official European Union Currency. It means that the value of one unit of Euro will be equal to the theoretical value of one unit of ECU on the first day. The mutual ratios of conversion between the participating currencies will be fixed on the basis of their market prices on the eve of the start of the currency union. It implies that the bilateral exchange rates between the participating currencies will be fixed on the basis of their market prices on that day prior to their commencement of the union, i.e.

December 31, 1998. These rates will be utilised for the calculation of the transgression of the values of the participating currencies into the single currencies. It can be presumed that the closing rates of exchange rates of the relevant currencies in the European forex market on the last day of December 1998 will solve as the anchor rates. As the day approaches some volatility in the European forex market may be seen and the respective central banks are expected to take care of that possible scenario. May be, the central banks will utilise their reserves of currencies to stabilise the values of the exchange rates.

The Interest Rates : ECU And The Euro : All the financial commitments denominated in old ECUs are expected to be converted into Euros when the single currency comes into being. Therefore ECU interest rates with maturities which overlap the monetary unions stuck up date will be affected by the weighted average of the interest rates of the component currencies as well as the expected interest rate of the single currencies. This is a possible scenario as the overlapping contracts cannot be avoided. If all ECU component currencies join the expected currency union simultaneously, the rate of interest applicable to all the participating currencies would converge to almost the same level and the theoretical ECU interest rate will also be comparable, because the latter will reflect the weighted average of the interest rates of the participating currencies. Because of this the start up of the monetary union will have no affect on the new Euro interest rate and thus the theoretical ECU interest rate will be an accurate guide to the level of prospective interest rate on the single European currency. If we assume that all the participating currencies will not simultaneously join the single currency union, the ECU interest rate will fail to provide a just anchor for the determination of the Euro interest rate. Therefore it will be logical to assume that the interest rates of the participating currencies will converge towards the interest rates market would think to be proper on the eve of the monetary union. Thus a probable problem is left to the operation of the market forces for its solution. In fact the proponents of the monetary union have been using this prospect as a stick with which to beat those opposed to the scheme that is speculative that the rates of interest of the non-participating currencies will become high by comparison with the rate of interest on Euro. If this situation becomes reality the theoretical ECU interest rate would rise above the actual ECU interest rate. The amount to which it does so is dependent upon the weighting the expected non-participating currencies in the ECU basket and on their expected differential against the participating currencies.

The Bank And The ECU : The ECU is a unique currency, as no central bank issues ECU and so there is no central bank to reconcile imbalances in the money market in ECU. But some banks in Europe do handle ECU and they undertake a task of taking care of the disequilibrium in the money market of ECU. When shortage arises in the market, these banks create the requisite volume of ECUs by earmarking the necessary amounts of the component currencies, using the formula as in Table 1. Again when surplus emerges, they absorb the ECU from the market by unbundling the ECU amounts into their components parts in terms of national currencies. These banks are basket makers. The latter extends a credit in ECU and they convert that by borrowing the appropriate components of currencies on the money market. When the demand for ECU credit exceeds a buy, the actual ECU rate of interest will be higher than the theoretical one, giving sufficient scope to the basket makers to have a large spread in their credit transactions. The basket maker takes an exchange rate position between the basket and the ECU, assuming the risk implicit in this on the belief that the rate of exchange rate of ECU will always return to its theoretical value in equilibrium. This may or may not happen and sometimes the basket makers face trouble to square their position.

Historical Perspective Of ECU : The European concept of a single currency has its origin in the attempt towards economic integration of Europe suggested in the Treaty of Rome, but the idea crystallised during Hague Summit of European leaders in 1969 and a committee was formed for a study for the feasibility of the creation of an economic and monetary union in Europe. The committee was headed by Pierre Werner, the then Prime Minister of Luxembourg and the committee published a report in October 1970, known as Werner Report. The report contained the conditions thought to be necessary for the monetary union in stages by the year 1980 and these were : (i) the concerned countries should give the reliable assurance that their currencies will be totally convertible; (ii) there should be complete liberalisation of all categories of capital transactions and the full integration of the banking and other financial markets among the member countries; and (iii) there should be the elimination of margins of fluctuations and the irrevocable locking of exchange parities. In March 1971 the EC member countries endorsed the Werner Report and they expressed their desire or political will to establish an economic and monetary union (ECOFIN Council Resolution, March 22, 1971). Despite political endorsement of the objective European Monetary Union the Werner report was not implemented due to economic difficulties, though the under current for the union remained strong.

At the Bremen European Council meeting in July 1978 a proposal for the creation of the European Monetary System (EMS) for the monetary cooperation among the member countries for the stability of Europe was accepted. The proposal also included the introduction of the European Currency Unit (ECU), which was to be used as the common denominator for the determination of exchange rates of the currencies of member countries. It was mooted that within two years of the establishment, the European Monetary Fund would be established, which will help the full utilisation of ECU as a reserve instrument and also as a means of payment. Though EMF was not established, the European Monetary System increasingly asserted itself and led to a tremendous increase in the monetary policy coordination among the members. In February 1986 the members signed Single European Act and EMU began to be recognised as a natural consequence of the commitment to create a market without political frontiers. The European council reaffirmed its earlier resolve for the creation of EMU. At the Hanover Summit in June 1988, Jacques Dalors, the President of the European Commission, was requested to study and make concrete suggestions for the establishment of the European monetary union. The report of the committee known as the Dalors' Report was endorsed in June 1989. The report envisaged three stages that would lead to the culmination of European monetary union. The three stages are :

(i) In the first stage the single market is to be completed, capital controls are to be lifted and measures should be adopted to reduce the regional disparities within the European union. Increasing macro-economic policy coordination by the Council of Finance Ministers (ECOFIN) were suggested. Further, the committee of Central Bank Governors should monitor the movement of the exchange rates of the member countries so that the movement is contained within a narrow band of the Exchange Rate Mechanism. The first stage should start by July 1, 1990.

(ii) In the second stage the European System of Central Banks (ESCB) will be established and the member countries should achieve the fiscal and monetary convergence of the system based on price stability. They should also see the stability of the exchange rate realignment. The ESCB will carry the task of the Committee of Central Bank Governors. The starting date for the second stage was specified as January 1, 1994 in the European Summit at Rome in October 1990.

(iii) While the stage two would see the establishment of the European Monetary Institute (EMI) which is the forerunner of the European Central Bank, the third stage requires the beginning of full monetary union. It begins with the irrevocable fixing of exchange rate parities between the currencies of participating member countries. Further the European System of Central Banks (ESCB) will assume full responsibility for the conduct of monetary policy. Monetary and foreign exchange rate policy will be carried out by the authority in the single currency. The Treaty of the European Union, i.e. the Maastricht Treaty resolved that the third stage will start on January 1, 1999. The Maastricht was signed in February, 1992 and ratified by the member countries in subsequent months. Though some countries have refused to ratify through referendum. The Treaty represents the legal basis and procedures for moving to full economic and monetary union and the introduction of single currency, ECU. The Treaty seeks to organise the member states and is quite explicit on this objective. Further it specifies certain requirements and timing for the aspects of stages two and three as mentioned above. The contents of the Treaty and its intent are summarised in the Annual Report 1995 of Bundesbank :

"In December 1995 the European Council agreed to adopt a name Europe for the future European currency and expressed the view that monetary union, subject to the achievement of a sufficient degree of convergence should start at the beginning of 1999. At the same time, the European Council agreed on certain major basic rules for the transition to the Euro. This so called change over scenario sub-divides the time required for completely replacing the national currency by the Euro, into three phases. An interim period lasting about a year, which will begin as soon as the decision is made on which Member States qualify and during which notably the European System of Central Banks is

to be set up and the concluding conceptual and technical preparation for Stage Three are to be met, will be followed from 1st January 1999 by a phase lasting upto three years during which a single currency will be introduced progressively for book entry transactions. A period not exceeding six months is specifically envisaged subsequently for the issue of bank notes and coins denominated in Euro and for the recall of national monetary tokens. If this phase does not already begin within the aforementioned three year period, it will start on 1st January, 2002 at the latest."

The long quotation underlines clearly that people behind the European Union do mean business.

The introduction of single currency will require some basic infrastructure and the European Monetary Institute has arranged some steps for that. First to enhance the credibility of the single currency the interbank money market and the foreign exchange market should switch over to the new arrangement simultaneously. For this change over during the transition phase the Trans European Automated Real Time Gross Settlement Express Transfer (TARGET) system is being prepared for the purpose of ensuring efficient conduct of monetary transfer among the member countries.

The Single Currency ECU And Other Arrangements : Among the members of the union preparations are under way for the change over to the single currency Euro on January 1, 1999. Starting on these dates the European System of Central Banks will conduct its monetary policy in Euro and the member states of the union will denominate their new Government securities issues in Europe. Latest by January 1, 2002 when the Euro bank notes and coins have been introduced and general government agencies have made the change over to the Euro, all retail banking activities will be conducted in that currency.

Meanwhile during the third phase i.e. from 1999 to 2002 banks will be dealing currencies in two spheres–with the Euro denominated markets on the one side and the world of retail transactions in the national currencies on the other. At the points where two types of currencies meet and overlap, the financial intermediation of the banks will play the vital role of interface and thus banks will be an important driving force in the change over of the markets to the Euro. The currencies dealers will enable the banks to meet the demand for Euro from non-financial agents and help them integrate transactions on markets where the quotation and settlement systems operate in Euro, into an economy where the national currency will be there in use. The financial institutions will assist the banks in the job. While the change over in the financial market will start on January 1, 1999, the change over in the stock of securities and transactions will be gradual.

The Foreign Exchange Market : Starting from January 4, 1999 the foreign exchange markets are said to change over to the Euro. This means that all non-Euro area currencies will be quoted against Euro only. This will ensure continuity with the practices on the ECU market, where the rates for all currencies including sterling are quoted against the ECU. Simultaneously the foreign exchange holdings of the institutions in Euro area currencies must be converted into a single currency and the settlements arising from the interbank foreign exchange market will be made in Euro. The derivative products like swaps, futures and options on Euro area currencies will automatically be converted with the substitution of the Euro for the national currencies of the Euro area countries. The change over to the single currency Euro will depend on the rules regarding the benchmark exchange rates which have to be worked out by January 1, 1999. The Central Bank of France publishes daily benchmark rates for the French franc against other currencies.

These rates are used for accounting and prudential purposes. Such benchmark rates will be required even after January 1, 1999.

There should be rules to be devised for the creation of a unified foreign exchange market for the whole Euro area which will be an incentive for the harmonization. Further rules are to be framed for dealing with open interest in currency futures and swaps on currencies for the non-European countries. The final value of such contracts should be known for certain by December 31, 1998. On the basis of that information a cash settlement price can be worked out on the basis of the differences between the rate originally contracted and the fixed conversion rate that is ultimately set. The questions which remain are whether contracts should be liquidated or whether such contracts should be allowed to run till they mature. The working groups are studying these aspects at present.

The Money Markets : The change over in the money market is expected to be swift. On the interbank market the change over will be facilitated because starting from January 1, 1999 monetary policy transactions will be conducted in Euro. Also the accounts of the banks with the central banks will be held exclusively in Euro and the large value payments system will also operate in Euro. The TARGET system will then be operational and it will handle all monetary policy operations and payments in the interbank transactions, it will also ensure smooth circulation of central money. On the negotiable dates security market the outstanding government bonds in multi ple currencies will be converted into Euro immediately. The technical process of converting other dead securities will not be a problem as most of them are short term securities held by credit institutions. The holders of the securities have to convert them into Euro denominations so that they can be used as homogeneous instruments.

The European Monetary Institute will contribute to the realisation of the conditions necessary for the transition to the single currency system. The ways it shall do are the following : EMI should strengthen the coordination between national central banks so that the latter coordinate the monetary policies of the member states with the aim of pursuing price stability. EMI should monitor the functioning of the European monetary system and hold consultations concerning issues falling within the competence of the national central banks. EMI should take over the activities of European Monetary Cooperation Fund which will be dissolved and it should facilitate the use of the ECU and monitor its development. EMI should also innovate instruments and procedures which are necessary for carrying out a single monetary policy in the third stage and it should prepare the rules for operations to be undertaken by national central banks within the framework of the European System of Central Banks. With consultation it should help in the adaptation of monetary policy instruments and their preparation of the procedures of carrying out the single monetary policy in the third stage.

The New Environment : After the take over of single currency on January 1, 1999 it is expected that the short term interest rates will be the same throughout the Euro area. Entry into the monetary union will be conditional on macro economic convergence, irrevocable fixing of exchange rates, a single monetary policy and also uniform fiscal policies conducive to the price stability. This all imply that macro-economic factors influencing the value of financial assets should be more uniform. Moreover, the subsequent subscri ption between financial assets within the same categories should be easy though the issuers are of different nationalities. This will have large impact on the interbank deposits, as the single monetary policies within the Euro area implies that the banks should offer the same interest rate to all clientele irrespective of their country of origin.

There will be some theoretical impact on the credit risk premium as the traders will distinguish between the creditworthiness of two sovereign issuers if they feel that risk of default is not the same in two cases. The assessment of the government as a credit risk is based on the estimate of how sound its financial position is. The factors determining that creditworthiness or the growth of GDP, inflation, balance of payments, the nature of the fiscal balance and the government debt. These factors will also determine the creditworthiness of the member countries and also they would be members who want entry into the union.

Impact On The Forex Market : The existence of an exchange risk induces the demand for additional premium and this extra premium upsets the losses that could be incurred due to a change in the exchange rate. The exchange risk between various countries entering stage three of the monetary union will disappear on January 1, 1999 as Euro takes over and fixed rates exists immediately before that. Therefore the yield differentials between these countries's securities reflecting the risk premium should be disappearing. Like the leading currencies of the Europe, the Euro should be as strong as that. Only then it can act as a magnate for savings from non Euro countries. In that scenario a large and liquid market of European government securities will be expected to emerge as an alternative to the investments denominated in U.S. dollar. The disappearance of exchange rates will lead to reallocation of portfolios as the managers will try to expand from domestic markets to Euro area countries. A major source of risk in investing in foreign markets within the Euro area will be eliminated and the disappearance of interest differentials will bring more homogeneity in the asset prices. The restructuring of interest rate product portfolios will help maintain yield differentials on various Euro area government securities. Because the bond markets will appear to be good substitutes for each other once the monetary union becomes a reality, there will be risk that the reallocation of cross border investment flows could favour the markets with attractive pictures. The differences in the technical features in government securities within the Euro zone will explain the yield differentials of government securities.

References

Bank for International Settlements, *BIS Review,* different issues.

International Currency Review, different issues.

European Monetary Institute, *Annual Report 1995* (Frankfurt, April 1996).

European Monetary Institute, *The Change over to the Single Currency* (November 1995).

APPENDIX B

INTERNATIONAL CAPITAL FLOWS AND ASIAN CURRENCY CRISES

MONEY HAS A GEOGRAPHICAL CONNOTATION and this aspect of money becomes prominent when a particular country becomes open in the sense that its domestic market establishes a link with the world financial system based on the policies of the domestic authority of the country.The latter influence the degree of the strength of the link. Taken as a whole this defines the organisation of the country related to the monetary system. Professor Arrow 1974) defines organisation as: Formal organisation, firms, labour unions, universities, or government, are not the only kind.Ethical codes and market system itself are to be interpreted as organisations; the market system, indeed, has elaborate methods of communication and joint decision-making. (p 33)

The market system as a part of the organisation is also characterised by uncertainty and all the dynamics associated with it. This aspect has become important in today's world of derivatives, as the latter exploit the virtues of uncertainty based on the applications of probability distributions.The Asian crisis which started in July, 1997 is a case study of the dynamics of market system as described.

The last quarter of 1997 had seen turmoil in the Asian Financial Markets starting with Thailand and coming to South Korea in the end. The crisis unfolded during 1998 as countries like Indonesia, Malaysia and South Korea started the revealations of the weakness of their financial system.The question is– what went wrong? The Asian crisis shows a variety of symptoms like a fall in exchange rate and also a fall in equity markets. The quantum of the fall is not unique in history, as Australia experienced a 35 per cent fall in exchange rate in the middle of 1980s and another 25 per cent in early 1990. In Japan also yen depreciated between April 1995 to April 1997. The depreciation of exchange rate may have been a trigger which set off a chain reaction of other events in the financial and real sectors. But left to itself the exchange rate changes would not be a crisis. The problem becomes a crisis when the weakness in the exchange rate infects the financial sector and this may happen through a number of channels. In some cases banks may borrow heavily in foreign currency and lend to the non-bank business sector. When the domestic currency depreciates, the increasing foreign exchange obligations push the corporate sector in crisis, they default on their debt to the domestic banking sector. At the same time the foreign lenders realise that a fall in exchange rate increases their credit risk and thus they pull credit lines or they fail to roll over short term debt. If the financial system is already having fracture lines and structural tensions, this type of exchange rate shock can bring crisis. There may be a number of weaknesses which are interconnected–government directed loans, poor credit evaluation, lack of transperancy and inadequate prudential supervision. So long as foreign capital inflows are sufficient and a high growth in GDP is maintained, the situation can remain sustainable. But the situation goes in reverse gear when confidence becomes fragile and capital flows become reverse. And the sudden surge of demand of foreign exchange (as domestic currency is to be converted into foreign currency) cannot be met out of forex reserve creating a helpless situation.

The above is a stylised descri ption of a typical South Asian economy which closely mirrors the reality either in Thailand or in Indonesia or even elsewhere. The countries in this region have been high savers, budgets have been balanced or in surplus, inflation has been reasonably low and exports have been a dynamic driving force of economic growth. The countries had high current account deficits, as they were investing much more. The financial sector was flourishing and the open capital markets ware a merit-badge of economic maturity and requirement for entry into the rich nations' club OECD. Globalisation and free flow of capital were embraced eagerly and the equity markets experienced growth as the complex products of Wall Street were readily available. International agencies urged faster deregulation, the commercial financial interests were eager to curve out a role for themselves in the fast growing sector and there was a craze for sophisticated financial products. The economic agents were often seen using the products without knowing the full implications. This happens during the phase of the transition from a regulated financial system to a deregulated one. Under the best of circumstances it was going to be accompanied by false starts. The pace of growth of credit is difficult to evaluate in a world where the expectation is that it is growing quickly as the financial repression is ending. This transition leaves the financial system fragile in the beginning. Thus the financial institutions were involved in excessive lending because of competition.

Where is the role of prudential supervision? For the prudential supervisors there was the classic case of the dilemma: where to blow the whistle on the problem and preci pitate a crisis or do work behind scene quietly and try to avert the perceived problem in the expectation that it will be rectified meanwhile. No credit is given for preci pitating a crisis early, but there is plenty of blame of being present at the scene of the crime. Seeing the spate of crises one by one, it is natural to have doubts about the efficacy of the supervision system.

South Asia's Integration To Global Market Some countries in South and East Asia have exhibited a rapid growth of exports and a quicker pace of integration in the global market. If we define the openness of the economy to international trade by the ratio of merchandise trade and the gross domestic product, Indonesia achieved 42.6 per cent in 1993 compared to 34.6 per cent in 1973, Philippines 55.2 per cent against 36 per cent, Thailand 66.4 per cent against 33.5 per cent, and Malaysia 144 per cent against 69.4 per cent during the same period. This growth is to be seen against the fact that the degree of openness of the 15 middle income countries was 38.7 per cent in 1993. This type of opening the economy may be related to the philosophy of exports led growth, or the decision of the political authority to bypass the difficult structural reform problem within the economy but again to have a high growth rate through globalisation.

The Surge Of Capital Flows The growth in international capital flows in recent times is the result of greater financial liberalisation and sophistication in the financial markets of many countries outside the OECD. Also the rise of institutional investors such as mutual and pension funds, growing financial innovations and intermediation in a derivative products and information technology have helped the process. But this capital flows can be very volatile in nature, with the tendency of reversing direction when there is the slightest hint of risk, whether it is the conduct of macro-economic policies, or the apprehension over the fragility of the financial sector. Capital flows then drive the balance of payments more than trade flows and portfolio shifts operate on the basis of market expectation of risk, return and liquidity. Further a high level of arbitrage operations lead to a contagion effect. Losses in one market thus result in sales in another market and the contagion effects spread across political boundaries quickly.

Asian Development And Its Uniqueness The 1990s witnessed huge capital flows toward the Asian region. According to IMF, average annual net capital inflows to developing countries exceeded U.S. $ 150 billion during a period 1990 to 1996. Of this amount more than 40 per cent came to Asia. In some Asian economics net inflows of capital have averaged 5-8 per cent GDP over long periods, and half of such capital flows are in the form of foreign direct investment. Asian economies also exhibit a large volume of liquidity. Of the total international reserve of U.S. $ 1500 billion,Taiwan, China, Hong Kong and Japan together maintained more than 30 per cent of the total international reserve. Also the accumulated international debt of the countries in this region is phenomenal. Apart from the liquidity aspect, Asia has become the fastest growing region in the world recording growth rates of about 5-9 per cent per annum. The inflation rates are low and exchange rates were stable until recently. The countries have high saving rates of about 30 per cent of GDP. Official savings were even higher in terms of foreign currency reserves and five of the top six foreign exchange holders in the world are now Asians.

The economies in Asia started experiencing high growth with the strong fundamentals–an educated flexible work force, stable political environment, good natural resource and communication infrastructure, openness to trade and high savings. These have not changed. Asia is still outward looking with open markets and openness to innovation. In this context we can consider the recent Asian market turbulence in the global context. Until recently Asia enjoyed the benefits of high global liquidity and recorded large levels of capital inflows as driven by high global liquidity in the top industrial economies. The latter is also the consequence of strong productivity growth, low inflation and improved government savings in the industrial countries which has resulted in strong growth in the world trade. With well behaved inflation the international liquidity has resulted in the global stock market boom in the 1990s in both Europe and U.S.A. and also in the new markets in Asia. But this has also caused a global compression of interest rate spreads and record levels of new issuance in both domestic and international markets. Such a narrowing of spreads did not reflect to potential credit and market risks associated with the new emerging markets in Asia. Thus when the investors realise that the emerging markets are carrying more risk than they have assumed, the risk premium as measured by the yield spreads will widen sharply to reflect this. When the spread is unable to contain the risk, flight of capital takes place due to portfolio movement.

The above scenario has been complicated by the fact that the flood of global liquidity has been channeled to the bond, equity and property markets of East Asia. Encouraged by the optimism about the Asian miracle growth, both the domestic and foreign investors committed the classic "fallacy of composition". Initially each individual investor may perceive a high return and increase their investment in assets, and this will lead in aggregate to excess demand and in market overshoot. A reversal of perception leads to a sharp market correction, and this is exactly happening in Asia and also in some parts of the world. One can say in retrospect that more investment money had flowed into these economies than could profitably employed at modest risk.

If we identify real issues in Asia as one of structural competitiveness in the global economy and one which is caused by shifts in global resources then the spill over of the disequilibrium, either domestic or external, should happen by exchange rate changes. With fixed exchange rate regime, the adjustment comes through changes in the internal prices and especially changes in the asset market prices. But with a floating exchange rates there may be adjustment in both internal and external prices. Keeping this in mind the authority should cover six major aspects of future risk management for the nation as a whole : i) credible policies, both monetary and fiscal, should be applied consistently; ii) sound fundamentals like high saving rate, prudent fiscal and balance of payment position, high foreign exchange reserve and sound debt management should be sustained; iii) good supervision like maintenance of capital adequacy and liquidity requirement should be followed; iv) capital account liberalisation should be phased appropriately; v) a good financial infrastructure with an efficient payments and settlement system for domestic and international transactions should be evolved and vi) a non-distortive incentive structure both in taxation and regulations should be maintained that will minimise risk concentrations and leverage in the economic sectors. The essence is that prices should reflect the true information which the market system wants to convey.

The pain of adjustment in Asia is enormous. If we go by the experience of Mexico in 1994 then the cost will be in the vicinity of a loss of 12-15 per cent of GDP for the Asian countries. There is no way that the countries can dodge this issue. Only silver lining is that if these countries can pursue the reforms with determination and consistency, they will come out stronger within a short period.Till then the agonies of the reform and transition process will continue as had been experienced by Mexico and some other countries.

Reference :

Kenneth J. Arrow, The Limit of Organization, W.W. Norton & Co., New York, 1974.

NOTES

NOTES

NOTES